HOLDUP ON HOLINESS

The Disclosurc of Three
Canonized Apocrypha in the Bible,
Leading Unconsciously to Atheism.

REGIS EITEL N.

Holdup on Holiness: The Disclosure of Three Canonized Apocrypha in the Bible, Leading Unconsciously to Atheism. by Regis Eitel N.

Published by EITEL MEDIA INC.

www.eitelmedia.com

Cover by Regis Eitel N.

Picture by Roman Ziomka, from Pexel.com

ISBN: 978-1-0689841-1-2

Printed in USA

First edition

DEDICATION

To my Heavenly Father, Lord and God, Who blessed me with an amazing mother, Philomène M. Yaka, from whom I learned the true meaning of love through her incredible demeanor and the endless streams of kindness she showered on me on a daily basis. I have the greatest admiration for her, both for her incredible intelligence and her remarkable inner beauty. Throughout her life she was an unshakable force of resilience in the face of persecution and trials of all kinds. Always smiling and caring for others, she fully embodied the character of my Lord and Savior, Jesus Christ of Nazareth. As such, I am certain of the outcome of her destiny, as she declared to the doctor who told me in front of her that she had two terminal cancers. She looked him straight in the eye and answered him in a calm voice: "I will be with the angels, in heaven."

CONTENTS

PREFACE

Life is a wonderful adventure, full of challenges that can be turned into great rewards if approached correctly and from the right point of view. No one knows what lies ahead. But from a Christian perspective, it's a certainty that the day of evil will come. Therefore, one must be ready for it and be prepared to face the storm that is destined to challenge our faith. Prudence teaches us to learn as much as we can before that inevitable moment, to build the skills and momentum that will lead to success.

Born and raised without any particular Christian teaching, I came to know the Lord in primary school, but especially after watching a movie that completely changed my life, as I was literally bowled over by the character of the Lord. So much of what was shown resonated with me as what should be the norm, which I completely adopted. In fact, it was already my behavior, I just had the confirmation and justification to do it clearly. life took a different turn when death suddenly took my father away. I was then a young teenager and began to experience the taste of what the Bible calls the day of evil. Interestingly, that day seems to last longer for some, with an intensity that also varies from person to person. In my case, things just kept increasing in frequency and intensity: My mother became ill shortly thereafter and could no longer work, which hastened the entry into the world of work for my siblings and me. When I started my family a few years later, my mother, who lived with me, died of cancer, which she hid from me so as not to be a burden and thus to afflict me, leaving me completely devastated. As these episodes in my life unfolded, they drew me closer to the Word of God each time.

When I fully committed myself to my search for the truth and became a follower of Jesus Christ, it seemed as if my faith had to be quenched at all costs. If my life had been marked by hard turns, I now faced the steepest hill I had climbed since I was born. My family was torn apart and my whole life became the inspiration for the book I'm writing now, hoping to help others find greater success on the "cross road" that leads to eternal life in Jesus Christ: love as God Almighty intended.

The Lord said that His followers would be persecuted just as He had been. This is not to be taken lightly, as is everything the Messiah has said. I've been thoroughly persecuted and have lost just about everything, from home and family to work and friends. I've been completely isolated for years now, pushed back in every aspect of my life and forced to live on the fringes of society. Even though I bought them in legitimate shops, my computer and successive mobiles are hijacked and controlled by strangers; I'm followed in the streets by people who express all sorts of bad feelings towards me for no apparent reason. My manuscripts are often deleted or made unavailable by various means. There are so many aspects to the persecution, which goes as far as editorial bias, which completely changes the viewpoint of my manuscript and tries to give it a meaningless expression. For example, I write "there are good or sons of God", but the editor changes it to "God or sons of God", which makes the following statement meaningless: "evil or sons of the devil." When I explain that the theory of evolution is a legend, another paragraph is created and I'm asked to make some clarifications. My original text was: "Various stratagems are used daily to promote this scheme, such as the promotion of mythologies that have no basis in truth, yet are implemented by law enforcement agencies around the world. The theory of evolution is the obvious illustration of this pitiful reality." The editor started a whole new paragraph with "The theory of evolution" and asked me to give an example of the legends I was referring to. Bear in mind that I paid a high price, hoping that a legitimate company with good reviews would not fall for such nonsense. The reality is that more and more people are sticking with evil as we're getting closer to the arrival of the Son of Perdition on earth. We are approaching apostasy and a total rejection of Christian values, to live fully and openly in lawlessness. Then the Antichrist will be revealed, who will rule the whole earth with an iron fist and impose the mark of the beast on everyone.

Since I have been unable to find a trustworthy professional to properly proofread and edit my manuscript, in the face of such deception, I have decided to publish it as is, after doing my best to remove all typos and grammatical errors. I apologize in advance for the inconvenience that any error might cause, and I understand that feeling. But the message I have to get across is far too important for me to abandon my quest, which is constantly being delayed by all sorts of tricks used to prevent its publication. In one of the four manuscripts I've already written - all of which have yet to be self-published for reasons I've mentioned - I explained that it is a tremendous responsibility to speak and take a stand in the name of the Holy Kingdom of the Lord, because the implications are eternal. However, it's with this responsibility that I have decided to self-publish these books so that the truth can be revealed and people can be made aware of the various snares hidden in their path.

I believe that God Almighty, the Father of our Lord Jesus Christ, is in total control of everything and will glorify His Holy Name as only God can. In a future book, I will go into more detail about the persecution I've experienced for more than ten years now. However, through such authentic proofs of the truthfulness of the Scriptures, my faith continues to grow in many ways. So, the more I'm oppressed, the more I'm convinced of the truth and authenticity of the Bible. As I often say, persecution praises our obedience to the Lord and only confirms what is written.

God willing, as the Apostle Paul said in 2 Timothy 4:7, one day I too will say: *"I have fought a good fight, I have finished my course, I have kept the faith."* (ESV)

All Glory, Honor, and Praise be to our God, through Jesus Christ our Lord and Savior. Amen!

INTRODUCTION

"What a wonderful world," said the cantor about this creation that seems to have everything needed to grow and know happiness. It may seem that all of manhood is alike; in reality, however, our world is divided into two main factions, separated by their respective beliefs: the faction of believers, who abide by the Lord Jesus Christ's teachings, opposed to a group comprising those who are Jewish (holding to the teachings of Moses), and pagans, which are all other religions and philosophy. Because the Jewish community doesn't recognize Jesus of Nazareth as the Christ or the Messiah, from a Christian perspective, they live in error because God has already provided the way out of death eternal; even His salvation through the living Word He sent as promised through past prophets' reports. As such, Christianity is Judaism fulfilment; thus, anyone outside of it still lives in the darkness of ignorance.

In times past, God has allowed mankind to seek Him, attempting to discover the truth in various ways, though He never ceased to show who He is by providing the creation with all sorts of blessings. People of all times have followed either justice or unrighteousness, which brought about the two factions we have to this day. These, in essence, represent those seeking the truth and wanting to abide by justice and righteousness, as opposed to others who delight in injustice and enjoy legends of all kinds from the world. There is therefore a battle of influence for the truth to be revealed to all or concealed from most of the public. Such is God's account as opposed to the devil's.

The face of the earth is in constant renewal, as people are born every day in a world that is continually drifting away from God's law of love, even His commandments. Newer generations are thus less exposed to the truth of God and more prone to become part of the "legends faction." Manifold stratagems are implemented daily to foster that scheme, like promoting mythologies having no grounds in the truth yet implemented through law enforcement around the world. The theory of evolution is an obvious illustration of that pathetic reality.

There is only one explanation provided to mankind, elucidating our genesis until the future in eternity, offering manifold testimonies explaining the exclusive way for souls' salvation. It's through the Bible, a self-explanatory book comprising various past prophets' scrolls: starting with the Old Testament, a core teaching of the Jewish community; and the New Testament, which clarifies earlier teachings and reveals God's salvific plan for humanity through Jesus Christ of Nazareth. The Bible is therefore the cornerstone of Christianity, as it guides in all the knowledge needed to save one's soul from the coming wrath of God in a world turning away from His love. It's self-sufficient and provides different resources needed to grow in the knowledge of Jesus Christ and successfully walk in His footsteps. Its knowledge is from the Almighty God and lets anyone who dives into its truth be transformed into a new person. It changes the mind in such a way that one is seen as a new creature.

Because of its tremendous potential, those of the "legends faction" inserted false accounts—allegedly from a disciple of the Lord—along with other reports that were not God's insight, for they were not sent by Him, but rather were of men. Consequently, such reports create the confusion around the Bible and its various explanations, its authenticity, and the reliability of the Lord's teachings. In this misunderstanding, many of the "legends faction" use these stories to belittle the Bible's authenticity, such as in movies and atheist debates concerning God's existence, allowing them to also undermine Christianity's impact in the world; many seeking the truth finding it tiresome to understand within all this disharmony, what really pertains to the teachings that should save their soul, and often end up abandoning their quest for the truth.

An analysis of the Bible, its history, and the composition of its actual version reveal a scheme that is designed to create disbelief in most people, even those willing to walk as the Lord Jesus Christ commanded. That design is so subtle, not only does it work on many unaware, but it proves by its cunningness the reality of the truth found in the remainder and trustworthy accounts of the Bible. It shows this battle of Christians is not against mankind but, as it's rightly said by the apostle Paul to the Ephesians about the real adversaries of our faith who are challenging us in secret, as written in 6:12. *"For we do not wrestle against flesh and blood, but against the rulers, against the authorities, against the cosmic powers over this present darkness, against the spiritual forces of evil in the heavenly places."* (ESV)

Sadly, for centuries the various Bible bodies haven't yet voiced their indignation regarding such disgrace.

1 INCEPTION

In many aspects, becoming aware of this world is like settling in a new country. One must learn the ins and outs of their surroundings and use that information efficiently to be successful in any endeavor. Usually at around twelve years old, people start to acknowledge and be conscious of their existence as a human and the milieu in which one has a role to play. It is the same for a community, which grows in acumen as time goes by through its diverse interactions with others.

From Abraham and the patriarchs through various episodes in history, the Hebrew people settled in the land God promised afore time with a protocol to follow. However, their reluctance in abiding by God's commandments provided through Moses during their forty years spent in the desert after the exodus from Egypt, caused them to gradually be challenged by their neighbors, then completely overthrown and dispersed among the nations. The king Cyrus ordained the temple and city to be rebuilt, and a remnant was sent, once again as foretold and promised by God. The rebuilt kingdom of Judah hosted the Messiah's birth and then His death on the cross, thereby making atonement for mankind's sins. But after a few centuries, the kingdom completely disintegrated, and its inhabitants were again dispersed among nations for a very long time.

More often than not, homogeneity is what makes a social network, and the various interactions in the whole creation fall under the same principle. God created Adam in His image and interacted with him through His Spirit until Adam and Eve sinned. They were then hurled out of Eden to live on earth only, with no way to enter again. Their firstborn son, Cain, who killed his brother, Abel, experienced the same fate by being cast out of the presence of God. Such has been the principle verified throughout history in various accounts, which the prophet Isaiah clarified in 59:2 and is applied in our daily lives when we walk away from God's love. *"But your iniquities have made a separation between you and your God, and your sins have hidden his face from you so that he does not hear."* (ESV)

Surely God's Holiness can't stand our sins and therefore creates a separation between us. Because by our sins, we more resemble the devil's image than God's; the more we abide by that behavior, the greater becomes that gulf between us. By doing that, we're getting closer to the devil, who gladly will impart his wicked influence in our lives with all its detrimental consequences. Already in the desert with Moses, the Israelites showed an unwillingness to follow God's commandments, causing various turmoil. Yet they persisted in their way, in so much they all died in the desert and, with few exceptions, only their posterity entered the promised land. A similar action producing an identical result, the principle also applied to the Jews during the Lord's ministry. He told them, for they doubted who He was, as written in John 5:46–47: *"For if you believed Moses, you would believe me; for he wrote of me. But if you do not believe his writings, how will you believe my words?"* (ESV)

Many have perpetrated the traditions of their fathers by being idolatrous and not following the law God gave through

Moses. Consequently, such have weakened the kingdom until its complete disintegration, vanquished by their adversaries. Still today, that same reluctance to follow God's way is observed, as they persist until now for most of them do not recognize the manifold evidences left by the Messiah, attesting He is indeed that living Word of God promised aforetime. And since those who abided by Moses's law understood the truth and believed in Christ Jesus, those not believing are the ones who follow human traditions and are idolatrous, as it's written in Isaiah 29:13-14, ". . . *Because this people draw near with their mouth and honor me with their lips, while their hearts are far from me, and their fear of me is a commandment taught by men, therefore, behold, I will again do wonderful things with this people, with wonder upon wonder; and the wisdom of their wise men shall perish, and the discernment of their discerning men shall be hidden.*" (ESV)

And even the apostle Paul expressed the same opinion, admonishing Titus, as written in 1:13-14: ". . . *Rebuke them sharply, that they may be sound in the faith, not devoting themselves to Jewish myths and the commands of people who turn away from the truth.*" (ESV)

Though Judaism is the foundation upon which Christianity is based, remaining in that sole teaching has become obsolete with the advent of the Messiah. The principle here is simply what God ordained after their exodus from Egypt, as said the prophet Jeremiah in 7:23: ". . . *this command I gave them: 'Obey my voice, and I will be your God, and you shall be my people. And walk in all the way that I command you, that it may be well with you.*'" (ESV)

Moreover, the apostle Paul stated to the Romans in 8:9, "*You, however, are not in the flesh but in the Spirit, if in fact the Spirit of God dwells in you. Anyone who does not have the Spirit of Christ does not belong to him.*" (ESV)

Moses clearly stated a prophet like him would rise from among the Israelites and they must listen to Him. No one else has met the various prophecies about the Messiah's advent, nor abounded in unseen miracles like He did. God is Holy and, in His infinite wisdom, has prepared a way for those who love Him to be established in the ministry and serve Him forever. Those, however, who are reluctant with that same plan will be sifted through and purged from the creation. As is the Creator shall also be the creation; any unconformity will be removed to keep only what matches God's design. The prophet Samuel explained that principle to the king Saul per God's perspective: *". . . rebellion is as the sin of divination, and presumption is as iniquity and idolatry."* (ESV) (1 Samuel 15:23)

Two persons cannot walk together without agreeing. Additionally, the chief priests at the time of Christ's trial before Pilate clearly stated what was their obedience. Having an earthly king rather than God makes them subjects of the devil, as reported the apostle John in 19:15: *"They cried out, 'Away with him, away with him, crucify him!' Pilate said to them, 'Shall I crucify your King?' The chief priests answered, 'We have no king but Caesar.'"* (ESV)

Throughout history, man attempted to replace God's wisdom with his acumen, only to prove his submission to the devil. There's only one Way leading to the Father in heaven, and that's Jesus Christ of Nazareth. It's the plain truth, and no concession can be made about it: God has sent His Word for the world to be saved by Him. Those who believe will be spared from the coming wrath that will annihilate all who have rebelled against His commands. Therefore, all other religions or philosophy, though they please many by their tolerance to commit sins, won't save their souls. One must always remember the devil created all these lies simply to prevent mankind to abide by the truth, which is the only way to be freed from his wicked influence. So, any thinking that isn't the truth falls under the myriad of deceits produced by the devil, only to lock people in a mind prison when they believe. The truth thus is Jesus Christ, as He stated plainly to be the Way, the truth, and life that's eternal, as the apostle John reported it in 14:6. Take note of what He says after that: *"No one comes to the Father except through me."* (ESV) He didn't say, "No one goes to the Father," but rather "comes." Meaning the Father and the Christ are one entity, just as He told the Jews, *"I and the Father are one,"* in John 10:30, like to Philip in John 14:9: *". . . Whoever has seen me has seen the Father. . . ."* (ESV)

One may object by saying, The Bible is made of legends, and Christ never existed. All this is only fiction. Let's consider the matter quickly with some key facts.

Other than Judaism, no other religion can provide a clear and precise description of our world's inception. Scientists aren't able to demonstrate with today's acumen that it has been otherwise. The evolution theory hasn't provided the beginning of a proof in centuries. On the other hand, though often concealed to the public, around the world is the knowledge of a flood that wiped the whole earth. Sciences also attest all humans come from a single ancestor. Manifold Bible prophecies are still fulfilled to this day, while the reminiscence of the past can be observed around the world. To this day, archaeology continues to confirm the numerous facts that are reported in the Bible. Various writings outside of Christian literature corroborate its historical facts[1...5]; the Messiah is, for example, described by certain authors not of Christian obedience as being a usurper using tricks to deceive the audience. Such comments only prove that He was real to them and not a legend, as many are enticed to believe because time has elapsed. These comments don't question His existence but doubt the genuineness of the ministry.

Also, the rise and expansion of Christianity is per past prophecies, as reported by the prophet Daniel when interpreting King Nebuchadnezzar's dream. Manifold Christians were tortured in ancient Rome until they were asked to leave, authorities being powerless in front of believers accepting to be killed for Christ, who was recognized and celebrated as God in early Christian times.[6] These are real facts one can still discover with little research.

But the most obvious and tangible proof is the dynamic of our current time, which aligns with past prophecies and describes the hatred poured against Christ's name, Christians' persecution, and the global rejection of virtues to abide in evil, which is slowly and steadily being revealed to the masses. An analysis of discourses that people in a position of power utter often reveal that sad reality. Wording is more and more obvious and allows to see what's been implemented. Either people desire to discover the truth and will be convinced by the Bible's accounts, or they will otherwise always ignore evidence of the reality and use any opportunity as an excuse that justifies their living in sin and delight in mischiefs. There are only two kinds of persons on this earth: Good or God's sons, and evil or offspring of the devil. When God's seed abides in one, such has been predestined to be in the image of Christ, and all things good and bad will contribute to manifest that reality. Wherefore, the apostle Paul rightly wrote in his letter to the Romans in verses 8:28–29: *"And we know that for those who love God all things work together for good, for those who are called according to his purpose. For those whom he foreknew he also predestined to be conformed to the image of his Son, in order that he might be the firstborn among many brothers."* (ESV)

One who observes our planet with the Bible's perspective will see the evidence of its genuineness in the dynamic we perceive in our world today. If Jesus Christ never existed, why is His name so hated and forbidden in many places, especially in educational institutions? What are all these learners not supposed to discover? Why are Christians wronged worldwide? Aren't government leaders often examples of being cunning liars who regularly get away with their mischiefs, all elections usually being where their skills are presented to a population that's aware of their dishonesty? Doesn't it prove these are indeed subjects led by Babylon, mother of all abominations on the face of the earth? We may be accustomed to wrongdoings, but that doesn't mean we must abide by these beliefs, nor should we in any way caution such behavior.

There isn't and won't ever be any fellowship between light and darkness. Even if the whole world turns to become evil, one with the seed of God will resist and oppose evil influence until the end. We are in this world to grow in the knowledge of Jesus Christ and become a truthful duplicate of His behavior. Hence, we strive to increase our wisdom and progress in love, righteousness, justice, compassion, forbearance, etcetera. After all, we're called to be the salt of this world, meaning our conduct should bring that equilibrium, making the world manageable. But if we don't bring any influence, it's as if the salt added to the food has no taste. Such is useless and deserves only to be tossed in the trash bin. The Lord Jesus Christ brought light on earth and left a fragrance of wisdom, which is love. We therefore strive to maintain that bouquet, to remind others what He brought. Love is light, even God's Glory: such is wisdom. Walking away from it is hatred, which is the darkness or ignorance in which most of the world is soaked. Consequently, aside from Christianity, everyone is in darkness and subject to the devil's influence.

However, Judaism—though falling in the group of those not following God's voice, thus His commandments—have a different status that will save them in the latter days because it's written God doesn't repent of His gifts and calling. The apostle Paul explains that mystery in Romans 11:28–32: *"As regards the gospel, they are enemies of God for your sake. But as regards election, they are beloved for the sake of their forefathers. For the gifts and the calling of God are irrevocable. For just as you were at one time disobedient to God but now have received mercy because of their disobedience, so they too have now been disobedient in order that by the mercy shown to you they also may now receive mercy. For God has consigned all to disobedience, that he may have mercy on all."* (ESV)

Does this mean anyone can sin willingly and will be forgiven afterward? Not really so! It's written in Revelation 21:7–8, "*The one who conquers will have this heritage, and I will be his God and he will be my son. But as for the cowardly, the faithless, the detestable, as for murderers, the sexually immoral, sorcerers, idolaters, and all liars, their portion will be in the lake that burns with fire and sulfur, which is the second death.*" (ESV)

Though many of the Israelites went astray, worshiping other gods—the alleged star of David is clear evidence that was even reprimanded in time past, as recalled Stephen in 7:43 of Acts of the Apostles, which reminds of Amos's prophecy found in 5:26–27: "*You took up the tent of Moloch and the star of your god Rephan, the images that you made to worship; . . .*" (ESV)

There is still a remnant of true worshipers who seek God with their whole heart and are sincere in their piety. Just as it was in the times of Lot in Sodom and Noah with the flood, only a small fraction will be spared. Isaiah in 4:3–4 prophesied about what will happen then. "*And he who is left in Zion and remains in Jerusalem will be called holy, everyone who has been recorded for life in Jerusalem, when the Lord shall have washed away the filth of the daughters of Zion and cleansed the bloodstains of Jerusalem from its midst by a spirit of judgment and by a spirit of burning.*" (ESV)

It's that remnant that will be spared when God's wrath is poured on all who have not obeyed His voice, rather have enjoyed injustice and have lived in hatred. All other religions fall in the category of the devil's deceits and will have no way out. What then about those who never heard the Good News of Christ? Romans 2:12–15 reads, "*For all who have sinned without the law will also perish without the law, and all who have sinned under the law will be judged by the law. For it is not the hearers of the law who are righteous before God, but the doers of the law who will be justified. For when Gentiles, who do not have the law, by nature do what the law requires, they are a law to themselves, even though they do not have the law. They show that the work of the law is written on their hearts, while their conscience also bears witness, and their conflicting thoughts accuse or even excuse them . . .*" (ESV)

We all have an innate knowledge of justice and righteousness, and God knows what are the intentions of each of us as He searches the hearts. We'll all be judged according to our deeds, though aims can be concealed to men. Besides, the day of evil is set to fall on all who dwell on the face of the earth, forcing anyone to choose between righteousness and lawlessness. Turmoil and difficulties come in everyone's life to define that status, in such a way that no one will be able to say, "I didn't know." Regardless of the circumstances of one's life, there will be a time in that existence that will clearly define the intentions of such a heart. It's written in Proverbs 16:4, "*The LORD has made everything for its purpose, even the wicked for the day of trouble.*" (ESV)

2 DELUSION

From the beginning of the creation, part of it abandoned its creator's law of love due to seeking personal glory. It all started with a highly ranked angel who used his hierarchical position to act as its owner. From the beginning, by means of various deceits, he progressively corrupted part of the creation, forcing it in subtle yet dreadful maneuvers to follow in his footsteps. The devil, that ancient serpent who once was a covering cherub perverted the first couple's thinking in such a way that they perceived everything upside down. Ever since, manifold have either followed their path or remained faithful to the Almighty God. The creation was made beautiful and peaceful, revealing love, which is God's nature, and He will restore it to its formal function. Meanwhile, all those who abandoned its initial modus operandi will be cast away in an eternal condemnation of death.

People are born every day, and because of the interruption caused by death, part of the knowledge they acquire is regularly lost. Even with the best intentions and dedication, a good part of the acumen people gain during their lifetime will be lost at the time of death. This implies not only that wisdom must be earnestly sought after, but such information must be truthful and productive to increase the reliability of what will be handed to the following generation. God is love, which implies that truth is the only way He operates. Truth is the reality, meaning what is real or exists. Thus, love can cause anything done with it to prosper or to exist: That's life. Yet God is also light, meaning a Holy Being, with no blemish whatsoever. Consequently, anything that comes closer to Him is enlightened, which is translated in abundance of life: Such one prospers in numerous ways. This means that when one acts per God's law which is love, the success of such enterprise is at hand. Applying another view will cause the adverse effect.

At all times, there have been good and bad people, striving respectively to get closer to or move further from God's law. Those walking per His commandments have the detriment to live in an environment greatly influenced by the devil's teachings and, more often than not, are fewer in number. Consequently, their battle to maintain the knowledge as per the truth is made even more challenging: Their surroundings' influence and death being the main boundaries upon which diverse deceits will add their share of hindrances, making the upright existence an eternal life pursuit. In His unwavering love, God has provided mankind with a book that collects the past prophets' scrolls, which allows an easy access to His teachings to maintain a good level of His law's knowledge and to sustain accuracy. All that is accomplished through the Word of God. For millennia, it has guided the people of God, starting with its prophets, then through the writings they left behind. Those were gradually collected by the Israelites. Then, after Christ's death, chronicles of the successive ministries of His apostles were collected by Christians and made available to the whole world. The Bible being the Word of God, its teachings enlighten whoever is exposed to it.

Because God is light and moving further from Him plunged mankind into darkness, this means with the sin of Eden, Adam and all his posterity were immersed in utmost ignorance. Because God is love and such is light and even wisdom, to believe in the devil and therefore doubting God's Word, Adam and Eve trusted lies as being the reality and thus considered truth to be a lie. Ever since, most of mankind follows that path, with a small fraction abiding by the ordained law.

To understand the effects behind that principle, it's important to comprehend the implications of light and darkness in one's life. God is not only omnipotent, meaning He has all power, but He is similarly omniscient: He knows everything—past, present, and future of whatever has, does, and will exist. Thereby, His knowledge has no limit. Because He operates only by the truth, He is Holy: Everything about Him is beyond what we humans deem impeccable. There is no defect or anything imperfect or not functioning properly with Him. That's the manifestation of life that's depicted in the first chapter of Genesis in the Bible. When God's light is expressed, existence is manifested and flourishes in numerous ways since life causes to be and brings about the existence of what is thought. In short, around God, everything prospers, flourishes, or expands. That's the effect of light.

On the other hand, its opposite, darkness, manifests the opposite effect, having all sorts of flaws and defects, ultimately ending in nothingness, in the torments of death. Light being wisdom and darkness ignorance, it's obvious one who is in darkness sees very little compared with those in the light. Wherefore, to counteract that drawback, the devil creates lies and foggy settings only the liar knows, making him look knowledgeable because he'll be able to bypass the various snares himself has disseminated and only he or his followers know. However, such knowledge is only partially entrusted to his disciples, otherwise he would no longer have any power on them.

Moreover, as ignorance prospers in foggy conditions, establishing the truth dismantles all its schemes. Imagine a moment that Eve, instead of eating, asked God if that was right: "We'll not die by eating the fruit of the knowledge of good and evil? Rather, our eyes will be open and we'll be like gods, knowing good and bad?" God would have probably been offended she had doubted His Word, but would surely have been glad she had asked for clarification. Undeniably, He would have condemned the serpent for creating such a messy state of uncertainty, which never exists with God: He is the truth, and the Word He utters is what's manifested always. Thus, she would have discovered they would have indeed had their eyes opened and known good and bad as gods, which they already were, as the dominion of the earth had been given to them. However, they would die, its fruit causing death to enter mankind, as it's the expression of darkness.

Death surely ends life on earth, but not only there. If man—understand both genders as they were made in Genesis 1, being created in God's image, is formed of a spirit, a soul, and then a body that allows to evolve on earth. As that physical envelope is discarded, the spirit and soul remain, and these are eternal. After being judged for their deeds on earth, they are either sent to live or to die eternally. And since these are spiritual entities, that death is similarly spiritual, even death of souls. This implies anyone on earth living aside God's commandments is spiritually dead, meaning living in hatred and not in love. Thus, they are ignorant meaning not aware of love and can't be part of the believers' faction sent to live eternally after their earthly death.

A battle of influence has always existed between God's children and the offspring of the devil. The latter, being in greater numbers, have often either precipitated or caused civilizations to end by their mischiefs and evil deeds. By corrupting the minds of people who gradually follow their trickeries, they invariably bring the extinction of these communities. Surely, death cannot cause existence to be manifested; rather, it extinguishes anyone that is. It is what we experience in our current epoch: The whole society is being perverted to its core, and everything that has established the current civilization is being distorted in such a way that youngsters learn a biased truth and are raised with the wrong values that will ultimately create a society that will auto-mutilate, then shatter. People will become eviler as time goes by, and they will simply reach a point of self-destruction. After eradicating the upright faction, to satisfy their lust for evil deeds, they will have no other option than to apply their harms to themselves, as they can't be at rest unless they injure someone. This can be verified by the previous civilizations who, after the zenith in knowledge, plunged into delusion, often attempting to create wealth and a wealthy society by launching various campaigns to conquer foreign lands. But even that deception never lasted beyond two millennia in the best-case scenario.

It's not the power that allows a society to stand, it's its values based on truth. Anything that is established on that foundation is made to prosper, like anything based on deceit is called to fail. It's that simple. Nothing good can emerge from evil, regardless of the cunningness of that scam. Lies may give an illusion of life and prosperity, but it remains a trickery. Thus, it's something that's not real or tangible. And it will inevitably return to its formal state after a certain period, proving its real value. In a world where children are taught God doesn't exist, yet witchcraft is presented as being the norm and often is arrayed in scientific terms, the notion of good and evil is reversed with numerous disastrous consequences.

For example, meritocracy isn't the way to succeed any longer; instead most people use privilege from veiled clubs they are part of. Favoritism has become so blatant in today's society, many enter these clubs in a quest for social status and a lifestyle they believe will be comfortable and fruitful, only to realize it's an ensnarement that will have a grip on their entire life and send their soul to death. Drugs are legalized despite the effects on people that have been observed in the past, and recognized as detrimental for the subject and its community. Howbeit, drug stores flourish like mushrooms, with effects to be gradually detected in the convulsion of our societies. If they were so fiercely combatted in time past, with the means used back then, why is it such today? Mankind hasn't evolved, and the facts remain what they once were. How many lives had been lost and regions devasted because of conflicts from drug dealers and armed forces? That is only one aspect of the divergence we observe today. If one commits murder under the influence of a drug, will it still be seen as such? With drugs having a devastating effect on people's nerves, is such a ruling in favor of our society's prosperity or its decline?

What is the projection made for tomorrow's society? The theory of evolution is taught to people, yet no proof of it whatsoever exists. Everything is actually organized for people to believe lies. Christmas is the most regarded celebration around the world, but it shares nothing with the Lord Jesus Christ. However, it's alleged to be His birthday celebration. Children learn this and believe Santa Claus and the remaining absurdities are real, only to realize later they were all lies repeatedly told by their parents—who are supposed to teach them lying is bad and must always be forbidden. What happens in the mind of a child who realizes those prohibiting deceits are actually masters in that category? Does this create an environment of trust and, consequently, adults who are confident because of their values being grounded in solid foundations? No! It creates a society led by perversion of all sorts as we observe today, as it has been foretold by the apostle Paul in his second address to Timothy per verses 3:2–5: "... *people will be lovers of self, lovers of money, proud, arrogant, abusive, disobedient to their parents, ungrateful, unholy, heartless, unappeasable, slanderous, without self-control, brutal, not loving good, treacherous, reckless, swollen with conceit, lovers of pleasure rather than lovers of God, having the appearance of godliness, but denying its power. . ."* (ESV)

Devices are used to foster schemes of witchcraft, and for many, it seems like a game, not perceiving the eternal consequences this will have on their souls. Halloween is another aberration by which many make their debut in devilry, and in all this, the Bible is called the lasting lie, and the Lord Jesus Christ is often depicted as legend. In this end times, truth has been arrayed as lie, while lies, legends, and various deceits are displayed as the reality. Having a society made of people who are ignorant and addicted to drugs, where promotion isn't given because of skills and abilities, but through allegiance to veiled clubs, is to raise a generation of slaves, just as it was in Europe when only nobles were learned and the peasants were considered slaves. The knowledge gap made lords stronger by their awareness and power due to their wealth, and the workers did not have much means to escape their miserable lives. Such is the context that is been re-created with now, the added practice of the past experience for those initiating these evil machinations, and making it worse by launching now this slavery system on the internet, allowing them to track every single movement. If in time past some slaves were able to escape and start a movement of resistance, this will be harder; thus, it shows the instigators of such naughtiness want to yoke people in unceasing bondage.

The only reliable historical book is the Bible, which covers millennia from our inception to our present epoch. Because this knowledge is concealed from most people, especially newer generations, such persons grow in an environment they find normal due to missing elements of comparison. But truly, it's getting eviler as time goes by, and it can only be detected with reports recording long spans of time like the Bible does. Otherwise, people have no reason to question the environment into which they live, as it simply seems normal, even if what is perceived as a little evil occurs here and there. However, these add up and, with time, lead mankind to the end of the world as we know it.

Therefore, knowledge is diluted in academies to weaken these learners, wrong information is provided about food nutrients, and people get into the habit of eating food that often causes illnesses in the long run—if even pets now have as much cancer as their owners, isn't it right there proof that food is the issue? Sugar is added to pretty much any nutriment, even salt. Yet sciences have proven an excess of that substance increases confusion, beside stirring up many other illnesses[9;10], as it weakens the immune system. Drugs surely add to this list a good share of troubles that don't need to be detailed here.

Our lives are run by the various celebrations that drive economies more than our intellect. These numerous celebrations inserted in each month of the calendar turn all those abiding them into aimless activity junkies. Made from legends, they have the sole purpose of keeping people busy thinking and running to and fro while their wealth is steadily sucked into a system that never has enough. All over the internet, on TV, and in movies, a lifestyle is advertised and various institutions incite consumption of their products, only to yoke people into loans they will spend their entire life paying off. When this seems out of reach, some enter veiled clubs that present the path of a life free from hassles of the current economic system. Since this is offered to teens without experience, they often embark on what will become the ride of their entire existence, bringing their worst nightmare to reality: slavery in a system that seems without exit.

Often, countries considered third world are scorned, yet their populace is thoroughly invited to relocate to allegedly wealthy countries with a salary indexation that's comparable to what they had in their own land. Surely, big cities in G7 countries look very much like third-world metropolises with their countless small businesses unable to provide a sustainable living for the owners. Many envy wealthy people, who always parade about in newer cars and pursue the latest trends without questioning the amount of the loans on their shoulders, nor do they question the requirement of the veil club that allowed such standing. Everything has a price, even if it's hidden, and especially from the public's eyes; it's not for the subject who knows exactly the cost. If many are praised for their thriving lifestyle, more often than not, the reality is completely different from what is displayed. Laughter and eccentricities are for the public that enjoys such entertainment. In private, when alone and facing reality, the attitude is different.

Surely, people have become accustomed to lies, and the system meanwhile offers solutions that seem too good to be true . . . and they are indeed what they look like. Even when dressed in beautiful attire, injustice remains unfair. It may be tempting because of one's circumstances; however, nothing happens in one's life by coincidence: there is always a purpose and an instigator. Various pitfalls were created in today's society, forcing people to consider veiled clubs as a place of relief. If financial institutions offer loans without waiting, interest is a reminder such luxury has a cost. Likewise, the so-called secret societies or veiled clubs offer opportunities during periods of challenge that appear like a relief, but there's a cost often not openly discussed, at least at the beginning.

Eternity is far too long, and one's soul is too important to jeopardize it with such trivialities of this ephemeral existence.

3 ESSENCE

The Bible, which has been both decried and revered, remains the only book able to stand the time test while providing an unmatched number of truthful reports. It is, in reality, the backbone of mankind's existence, as being the only book revealing a storyline spanning millennia. Some employ it to grow in wisdom and secure the salvation of their souls, while others abuse it to mislead and hinder others' success. Regardless of the goal, it has proved to be exceptional by its Author, the Almighty God; its composition, assembled throughout millennia from prophets of various locations; its genuineness, collecting an innumerable amount of prophecies and revealing unique truths about our world; its power, as being the mind of a Holy Being that enlightens whoever approach Him. Similarly, that book enlightens the heart of anyone diving into its wisdom and so much more that cannot be explained with words. Manifold attempts that failed to destroy it throughout history prove not only its importance, but also its uniqueness: It's the mind of the Creator of this world, sent to save the souls of anyone who believes in it.

The world comprises children of God and offspring of the

devil. While the latter are taught early in life, and consequently are very active and aware of their world, the former learn their status through various challenges in life. Consequently, if the latter are aware of their obedience, the former for a while aren't and must experience different life events to discover the faith in Jesus Christ. While still unaware, these are the persons who must be reached by evangelists to convert them and therefore allow their life to be fulfilled per God's plan. Even if not consciously aware, God's children have an innate desire to walk per their Creator's law of love, wherefore Grace often is already present in their life, as they naturally walk according to His commandments. When exposed to the Bible's knowledge, it's a revelation and the materialization of what they've always thought without being able to validate it. When God's seed is in one's heart, he intuitively knows the truth of God, which he will seek his entire life. That's simply how we are made. They can be wrong paths and various deceits along the way, but that will not quench the desire to know the truth. It's something in our heart we cannot satisfy until faced with the reality: the love of God.

There are numerous explanations about our existence, many doctrines that are as ludicrous and eccentric as they are perverted, yet none bring light, only confusion. To try understanding our existence on earth and what the Lord made available for us, let's imagine one arriving by plane in a new country. The instruction given to him is to take the taxi at the airport, and he will be transported freely to the hotel prepared for him at the appropriate destination. The name of the driver is Holy Spirit, and He is waiting in His car, a white automobile without bell and whistle. The taxi is parked in the waiting area with the code J7, and the only thing the passenger needs to tell the driver is, "I believe Jesus Christ, who was raised from death, is Lord at the right hand of God."

Once at the taxi stand, however, that customer will notice there are diverse taxis waiting to pick up clients. Many will approach him with different offers, but he will decline, knowing the driver waits in the car that came to get him. Others will show their cars with various flashing features, yet also will be ignored: The car is white and has no bell and whistle on it. The discussion with some drivers whose names aren't what's expected will likewise be discarded. In the midst of all this, a driver patiently waits until one says what's appropriate and is chauffeured as God planned. We are predestined by God to be in the likeness of the Lord Jesus Christ, and everything before our birth is organized by our Creator for our life to be successful. There will be challenges and times of disappointment and doubt. But with perseverance and the assurance that what has been foretold will be accomplished, we'll succeed.

As the truth is unique and consistent in time, unaltered since the beginning of mankind, the salvific plan made to save our souls remains the following: God created angels before humans, though they are similar in heavenly realms. The main difference is that the former are created to be in heaven and don't reproduce, while the latter are destined to temporarily reside on earth, populate it, and have dominion over every living being. A third of the angels forsook their assigned duties and followed the devil in a rebellion that will be rescinded by a new set of angels trained on earth to obey God, regardless of the conditions they encounter. Such are picked among humans and will be challenged throughout all their earthly life to be found worthy to serve God in heaven in replacement of the faction that rebelled. A plan is established and has a span of seven thousand earthly years, or days in heaven. That's what in essence is recorded in the Bible to guide all candidates throughout their mission.

God thought and provided His orders to angels, who conveyed them to prophets. These wrote them down, and that's what we have in the Bible today. Since it's God's mind, when one applies its wisdom in his daily life and believes it, that person has integrated the mind of the Lord Jesus, which is the truth. The apostle Paul said in 1 Corinthians 2:16: *"'For who has understood the mind of the Lord so as to instruct him?' But we have the mind of Christ."* (ESV)

Contemplating virtues has for effect to turn us into their likeness, thus, to worship God and dive in His Word change our mind into His, with all its implications: Since God is the absolute truth and Holy, thinking like Him implies success, prosperity, and abundance of all sorts, which is simply manifested through Grace in blessings. However, considering something else will also change anyone into its likeness, as it was for the Israelites of Ephraim who became idolatrous, as Hosea prophesied in 9:10. *". . . But they went to Baal Peor, And separated themselves to that shame; They became an abomination like the thing they loved."* (NKJV)

Essentially, those of the legend faction are all idolatrous, meaning they worship something else than God's Holiness, which simply is to abide by any of the multifarious lies of the devil. Consequently, they're changed in the likeness of the very thing they adore. If they're called sons of the devil, it's because their behavior reminds that of their leader. They are therefore two different factions, opposed by their respective convictions and aims during this earthly life, like in heaven are opposed those who remained faithful to their Creator to those who've rebelled, respectively helping believers and idolatrous to foster any endeavor meant and called to be in heaven. In His infinite wisdom, as God knows before the expression of a thought through creation, what will be its end, the salvific plan designed to save mankind has been hidden to angels until Christ's apparition on earth. In such a way it's now through the Church that those who rebelled learn God's infinite wisdom. Surely, if they knew how Christ would lay down His life for mankind's sins, they wouldn't have proceeded with such execution, because His atonement encapsulated all sins used to accuse believers before the Father in heaven. Wherefore, the devil has no longer even a single argument before the judge to request the condemnation of those who walk in Christ's footsteps. To overcome that helplessness in the face of fate, they planned to have these believers condemned by infiltrating the Church and corrupting its teachings. In such a way, either believer will sin unknowingly and then be condemned—because God is Holy and won't spare anyone walking away from His law of love—or believers will be enticed to sin and perverted in such a way, they will abandon the way of truth and become carnal-minded. That was the very trick used in time past with the Israelites in the desert after their exodus, as Moses reported in Numbers 25:1–3. "*While Israel lived in Shittim, the people began to whore with the daughters of Moab. These invited the people to the sacrifices of their gods, and the people ate and bowed down to their gods. So Israel yoked himself to Baal of Peor. And the anger of the LORD was kindled against Israel.*" (ESV)

Israel's enemies, unable to subdue them militarily, used deception as a tactic to weaken the people of God. Since their worship of the only True and Holy God made them likewise, as such, they couldn't be cursed—as the attempts to have Balaam curse them failed, having the people defile themselves to separate them from their Holy God and make them consequently vulnerable was the plan. Just as it worked with Adam and Eve in Eden, who were Holy and walked in love, having them believe in the devil's thinking separated them from God's mind. They lived with hatred and forsook love, aspiring to gain what had already been given to them—the whole earth dominion, which made them gods, as being children of God, led by His Holy Spirit, just as it was said of the Israelites who received the law and therefore were led by the Holy Spirit of God in John 10:34–36. "*Jesus answered them, "Is it not written in your Law, 'I said, you are gods'? If he called them gods to whom the word of God came—and Scripture cannot be broken—*

do you say of him whom the Father consecrated and sent into the world, 'You are blaspheming,' because I said, 'I am the Son of God'?" (ESV)

The perversion of the people of God in order to diminish their strength is therefore the way to subjugate them and in the end to destroy their souls. Their whole lives are centered on the knowledge of God's Word, to practice it as Moses in Deuteronomy told it should be, written in verses 6:6–9. *"And these words that I command you today shall be on your heart. You shall teach them diligently to your children, and shall talk of them when you sit in your house, and when you walk by the way, and when you lie down, and when you rise. You shall bind them as a sign on your hand, and they shall be as frontlets between your eyes. You shall write them on the doorposts of your house and on your gates."* (ESV)

As a matter of fact, the Church has been literally invaded by a herd of evildoers, having nothing to do with the Lord Jesus nor His teachings, but only seeking to make it crumble from within, as warned the apostle Paul before his arrest in Jerusalem, reported in Acts of the Apostles 20:29–30. *"I know that after my departure fierce wolves will come in among you, not sparing the flock; and from among your own selves will arise men speaking twisted things, to draw away the disciples after them."* (ESV)

Moses already before his death reprimanded the Israelites about such behavior in Deuteronomy 31:29. *"For I know that after my death you will surely act corruptly and turn aside from the way that I have commanded you. And in the days to come evil will befall you, because you will do what is evil in the sight of the LORD, provoking him to anger through the work of your hands."* (ESV)

Likewise, the apostle Peter will caution the disciples with his second letter sent to the dispersed in Babylon, as reads 2:1–3. *"But false prophets also arose among the people, just as there will be false teachers among you, who will secretly bring in destructive heresies, even denying the Master who bought them, bringing upon themselves swift destruction. And many will follow their sensuality, and because of them the way of truth will be blasphemed. And in their greed they will exploit you with false words. Their condemnation from long ago is not idle, and their destruction is not asleep."* (ESV)

In verse 2:14, the apostle Peter even depicts their conduct, revealed in the midst of congregations: *"They have eyes full of adultery, insatiable for sin. They entice unsteady souls. They have hearts trained in greed. Accursed children!"* (ESV)

Manifold false teachers have emerged, today more than ever. As everything is being turned upside down, they flourish in a season readily suitable for their mischiefs. Synagogues of the devil appear and grow at a continually increasing speed, even in times of crisis. Those challenged by life events and seeking enlightenment to properly address their situation, often are introduced to wolves not sparing the flock. And many lives are wrecked in merciless ways by some who have nothing to do in a church, most of them being sorcerers. Surely, many of these false churches are controlled and directed by veiled clubs behind the scenes. These alleged pastors are active members of these clubs, teaching doctrines of demons to innocent people unaware of their tragedy. A believer who is self-taught, however, will often escape their snare. Because when such ones seek the truth by learning the Word of God and are guided by the Holy Spirit of God, detecting false teachers and teachings comes easily.

In time past, as the Church became outrageously pagan, a fraction separated to develop what has become Protestantism, that revendicate a more appropriate Christianity, freed from pagan custom and brought back to its essence. After a period of turmoil, the various books of the Bible as we know it were assembled. It's supposed to have discarded all apocrypha and regained its originality. But is it the case? Throughout history, a pattern has often been observed, and such is discernible with many movements in today's actuality: False leaders are erected to lead a growing movement of contestation, only to lead such in what looks like a solution but is in fact a dead end.

In Europe, when people discovered the Bible, they were enlightened, and a movement seeking to establish a new way of living was calmly and cunningly muffled, turned in aimless pursue of social equalities never attained until this day. Likewise, today, many movements arise helped by the new way of communication: social media. Yet all these, like in time past, are just a pursuit of the wind and a wasting of time. The Bible hasn't been spared, and those pretending to work for its restauration and souls' salvation, actually labored for its corruption to threaten in the most evilness way, not only its reputation, its genuineness, its power to save souls, but also its knowledge.

Because the Bible is the Word of God, which doesn't require special training to grasp its teachings, and because it literally frees the mind of whoever dives in it, it is a real danger for our society based on lies and deceits. It teaches the truth from God, which allows to dismantle every single lie of the devil, thus making the world's lies fall flat. Because God's Mind is truth, as such, He not only can detect deceits, but it also provides the right path to be followed for success in any endeavor. It allows one to be coherent and therefore promotes success in any activity one will pursue. A knowledge of such quality that's offered to the public and is so powerful, if not controlled, can harm any scheme aiming to insidiously extricate people's wealth and possession of different kinds. It needed thus to be neutralized to avoid the system we're living in from being exposed and all their efforts to bring about a new era of slavery dismantled.

There are various ways to hide something that can't be hidden, for people not to have access to it. Some lands have banned the Bible's distribution and enforced this by law, with terrible consequences for any offender. In occident however, different methods are used, since human rights impose a certain comportment that officially must be observed. Therefore, rather than forcing people not to use that book, its depiction as legends is ventilated and debates are often planned to affirm it's a falsity. Since no proof could be exhibited to demolish its accuracy, some needed to be crafted, making such debates more balanced, as giving the "legends faction" means to promote their deceits with more authenticity. The Story of Matthew was consequently invented and inserted in the books as being the account of the Lord's disciple. Alongside were added the books of Esther and Song of Songs by King Solomon, son of King David. However, they do not have the acumen of the Holy and most High God, nor bring any enlightenment, but rather confuse, as being teachings of men and for most, an obvious work of the antichrist.

4 PRETENSE

Either people disguise the truth and make it look like something else, or they defile it in such way, those who should be interested will be repelled by it. In the case of the Bible, both methods are used: Campaigns of defamation are organized to wreck its reputation, while other movements labor at concealing its existence by pledging that the world was created by a cosmic accident. Thus, inserted between the Bible's manuscripts are stories without God's insight nor truthfulness, making the ensemble look discordant and much more like a scheme, which thus is accentuated by the ostensible wrong behavior of that part of the Christianity, having nothing to do with it as being pagans, even carnal-minded who have infiltered the Church, often self-proclaimed Christian entities, who display by their manifold mischiefs, what prophets and apostles have prophesied about the way of truth being blasphemed. Surely, these consciously act openly, knowing this undermines the image of the Bible and likewise of God, since they are all of the "legends faction", working in cohesion to throw the truth down to the ground. The case of the aberration wrongly titled the Gospel of Matthew is an incontrovertible example of these practices.

Does a teaching purpose set today's Bible four Good News stories' order, to allow an easy grasp? Even when following a Bible's education perspective, it seems illogical to have the actual Good News records order, allowing one's progression in Jesus' truth, making who's less knowledgeable to ingrain more easily, as the disciple. From Genesis to Revelation, through the prophets, God has taught deep truth, forcing the reader to seek a higher understanding in wisdom and understand the real connotation of things, always bringing a greater and broader understanding of His love, truth, and Justice, thereby teaching righteousness. Matthew's story contains many outlaw references, while John is the most theological, with Mark and Luke, respectively, progressing further in details reckoning Jesus ministry's events with the added Jewish background displayed with Luke's. However, no other book brings doctrines in complete contradiction with the whole Bible's teachings: Love is the truth and, thus, Holy.

Luke's credit comes from his long journey as the physician and closest friend of the apostle Paul, who is in turn endorsed by the apostle Peter; the report of Luke is more based on facts assessed by knowledge gained through his acquaintance with Paul, the author of more than fifty percent of the New Testament. Luke has introduced a comment at the beginning of his narrative, explaining how he put together his chronicle. It's evident the main source is the record from Mark, Barnabas's cousin, who assisted Paul for a season in his ministry, as written in verse 12:25 of the Acts book. *"And Barnabas and Saul returned from Jerusalem when they had fulfilled their ministry, and they also took with them John whose surname was Mark."*(ESV)

Paul, in a like manner, endorsed Mark, as written in verse 4:10 of a letter sent to the Colossians: *"Aristarchus my fellow prisoner greets you, and Mark the cousin of Barnabas (concerning whom you have received instructions—if he comes to you, welcome him),"* [ESV]

In his second letter to Timothy, Mark's experience again is referred to, in verse 4:11. *"Luke alone is with me. Get Mark and bring him with you, for he is very useful to me for ministry."* [ESV]

Mark, who also was trained as disciple of Peter who credited him in his first letter, as verse 5:13 reads, *"She who is at Babylon, who is likewise chosen, sends you greetings, and so does Mark, my son."* [ESV]

The author of the book labelled Matthew has no recognition from a known author of the Bible; he has no known past record. A perfect stranger, allegedly the apostle Matthew, yet without one single proof corroborating the pledge. The Matthew account can't be the Lord's disciple's report as some pretend. He couldn't be among the eleven apostles, hearing Peter's version of the field bought with the betrayal's profits as they were choosing Mathias in replacement of Judas, and still write this completely different and opposed version of such events. Moreover, since he was an eyewitness of the Lord and, better yet, one of the twelve, why did he need to duplicate the record of one who wasn't even among the disciples, and on top of that, add wrong references? Shouldn't, on the contrary, his report be more authentic, as the one of the apostle John?

The Lord said in His prayer none of those the Father gave Him was lost, but only Judas Iscariot. Therefore, Thomas's apocryphal account can't be of that disciple either, but rather some falsity credited to him to ground its legitimacy. Similarly, this record wrongly called Matthew can't be from an eyewitness to Jesus' ministry. It is, howbeit, the very one placed at the forefront of God's Word New Testament. His report, full of doctrines in total contradiction with the prophets and also other testimonies' authors, brings only confusion. Yet, such one is displayed as the introductory account of the truth's knowledge. Why? Who decided to have it included as one of the Bible's books and on which grounds?

It's impossible for the Bible scholars to have missed these errors.

And yet it's that one the Bible Good News' first testimony, though it's obvious such is from the latter to have been written. Not to discourse about its various inaccurate references, which are skillfully aimed at discrediting the Good News' doctrines and don't bring the known Biblical truth that acknowledges the Holy God's infinite Wisdom. As the Word of God's exactitude allows a mathematical reckoning of its references, attesting to Jesus' infinite knowledge. Because all is only truth, its references can be tracked back to their source. Men of all times have prophesied because the Holy Spirit prompted them to, as the apostle Peter said in his second letter in 1:21. *"For no prophecy was ever produced by the will of man, but men spoke from God as they were carried along by the Holy Spirit."* (ESV)

Amos wrote in 3:7–8, *"Surely the Lord GOD does nothing, Unless He reveals His secret to His servants the prophets. A lion has roared! Who will not fear? The Lord GOD has spoken! Who can but prophesy?"* (NKJV)

What's written by faithful servants and conveyed through the Holy Spirit is therefore the Word of God, and He is Holy. Any falsity will only bring confusion, which is the endorsement of the devil, proven since the Genesis with Eve. In that regard, this apocryphal of whatever is the real name of its author is only the work of the antichrist, denying the Lord's existence so subtly, it can't be uncovered unless guided by the Holy Spirit in a meticulous study of the Word of God. Anyone who will study the Bible, skipping for a season that record, will be amazed by God's light of truth because the whole scripture will become clearer and make perfect sense. Confusion is organized by sly factions taking advantage of knowledge gaps to create chaos and launch hidden schemes that harm the community in many ways. Such are those enticing to neglect the Word of God; they themselves use to hurt whomever heeds to them. God's Spirit rejoices in truth, but evil delights in the confusion and mischief. Lies of the devil aim to bring misunderstanding and foster failure, but God's Word, our Lord Jesus Christ, is the truth, bringing wisdom and success. Thus, the Word of God gives life, as it has been from Genesis and still is today.

Mark's, Luke's, and Matthew's accounts are akin, with a storyline that is almost identical. Given that Luke and Mark knew each other, as being close collaborators of the apostle Paul, it upholds the explanation Luke gave as the introductory of that narrative, stating in verse 1:3, *"it seemed fitting to me as well, having investigated everything carefully from the beginning, to write it out for you in an orderly sequence, most excellent Theophilus."* (NASB)

It appears evident Mark is the main source of Luke's report, having received that story while he was the assistant of the apostle Peter, who was one of the closest disciples of the Lord. Matthew's version, on the other hand, apparently follows the narrative of Luke's account, as both have a similar statement that's different from Mark's in 8:11–12. *"The Pharisees came and began to argue with him, seeking from him a sign from heaven to test him. And he sighed deeply in his spirit and said, 'Why does this generation seek a sign? Truly, I say to you, no sign will be given to this generation.'"* (ESV)

Luke, like Matthew, inversely states there will be only one sign, which is of the prophet Jonas, recalling the time he spent in the belly of a great fish, when he was fleeing to Tarshish. Luke 11:29 reads, *"When the crowds were increasing, he began to say, "This generation is an evil generation. It seeks for a sign, but no sign will be given to it except the sign of Jonah. For as Jonah became a sign to the people of Nineveh, so will the Son of Man be to this generation."* (ESV)

Matthew's story states it twice, of which verses 12:39–40 reads, *"... "An evil and adulterous generation seeks for a sign, but no sign will be given to it except the sign of the prophet Jonah. For just as Jonah was three days and three nights in the belly of the great fish, so will the Son of Man be three days and three nights in the heart of the earth."*

(ESV)

In chapter 16, it's written in verse 4, *"An evil and adulterous generation seeks for a sign, but no sign will be given to it except the sign of Jonah." So he left them and departed."* (ESV)

However, since Matthew's version also mentions a scripture found only in Mark's account, but isn't indicated in Luke's report, it's evident that the author of Matthew surveyed both manuscripts to forge his chronicle. This proves both reports existed already when Matthew's story was created. Mark 15:33–34 reads, *"Now when the sixth hour had come, there was darkness over the whole land until the ninth hour. And at the ninth hour Jesus cried out with a loud voice, saying, 'Eloi, Eloi, lama sabachthani?' which is translated, 'My God, my God, why have you forsaken me?'"* (NKJV)

Here are some deceits encountered in Matthew's report, with their implications explained for readers.

1. The genealogy of the Lord in the story called Matthew differs from the one provided by Luke, who started with God through Adam to Abraham, which section is omitted in the Matthew's story that starts only with Abraham. Until Hezron, diverging on two generations, then rescinding with Amminadab and his son Nahshon, to differentiate in the following generation. And after the fourth following generation, at the exception of Shealtiel the father of Zerubbabel, they won't be any convergence. Luke's genealogy is made up of godly kings quoted in the Chronicles of the Kings, whereas Matthew's lineage is often made up of ungodly kings, or whose names are found nowhere else in the Word of God. Thus, fourteen persons appear in both reports out of fifty-five, when starting with Abraham, or seventy-six if Luke's full lineage is taken into account. (Matthew 1:1–16)

2. The wise men or mages coming from the east because

they saw in the sky the star of the new king born isn't at all about Christianity and, thus, a Bible teaching. It gives the impression God has allowed man to seek signs in stars, which is quite the opposite. Isaiah, when rebuking the numerous idolators, prophesied in verse 47:13 as follows: *"You are wearied in the multitude of your counsels; Let now the astrologers, the stargazers, And the monthly prognosticators Stand up and save you From what shall come upon you."* (NKJV)

How could the Lord reproach Israel for making a star to worship with Amos, but through a record contradicts this teaching with wise men who inquire about a Jewish King whose star they saw? Even that star that led them to the place where the Messiah was? Amos's prophecy in 5:26 tells us, *"You also carried Sikkuth your king And Chiun, your idols, The star of your gods, Which you made for yourselves."* (NKJV)

Amos has a long, reliable list of prophecies having been fulfilled—not the author of Matthew, whose storyline is the copy of Luke's account, twisted with its various added contradicting doctrines that don't align with the pattern found in God's Word. So, it's dubious and leads me to inquire if this isn't an apocryphal account.

How could a star that is so far in the sky proceed before them? How did one star travel in the sky while others around it didn't? Was it a shooting star? Moreover, how could an object that far away pinpoint a location on earth? (Matthew 2:9)

Throughout the whole Bible, God speaks in dreams only to righteous ones, never to idolators or sorcerers, etcetera. They communicate with demons, which explains why Joseph in Egypt and Daniel in Babylon were able to provide God's explanation of dreams that sorcerers, magicians, astrologers, and Chaldeans could not. So was it with Daniel giving to the king Belshazzar the explanation of the writing on the royal palace's wall. Yet in this instance, this story's author pretends it's otherwise. Hence, it's the only one in the whole Bible.

(Matthew 2:12)

3. He's the only one speaking about the Lord Jesus' sojourn in Egypt, yet that is something God often asked in the past to avoid, rather to set expectations on His salvation, not on men. To have it in Jesus' story induces the thinking of God not being able to properly protect His own Son, rather counts on the strength of the devil by his subjects, the Egyptians. It's reported by Isaiah in verse 30:3, *"Therefore shall the protection of Pharaoh turn to your shame, and the shelter in the shadow of Egypt to your humiliation."* (ESV) Yet in verse 30:7, Isaiah continues by saying, *"Egypt's help is worthless and empty; therefore I have called her 'Rahab who sits still.'"* (ESV)

Ezekiel also prophesied about Egypt in verse 23:27 which states. *"Thus I will make you cease your lewdness and your harlotry Brought from the land of Egypt, So that you will not lift your eyes to them, Nor remember Egypt anymore."* (NKJV)

Finally, he says in verse 29:16, *"And it shall never again be the reliance of the house of Israel, recalling their iniquity, when they turn to them for aid. Then they will know that I am the Lord GOD."* (ESV)

Jeremiah said it plainly to the remnants of Judah in 42:19, *"The LORD has said to you, O remnant of Judah, 'Do not go to Egypt.' Know for a certainty that I have warned you this day."* (ESV)

All these were prophesied afore the Christ advent; would then the Lord go against His own previous orders? *"Out of Egypt I called my son"* is a statement that applies to Israel, even God's chosen people, and never to the Lord, as written in Hosea 11:1. *"When Israel was a child, I loved him, and out of Egypt I called my son."* (ESV) No wonder much isn't said about His sojourn in Egypt, other than Joseph asked in a dream to leave the land.

4. The rhetoric in the Matthew story is more about the Kingdom of heaven rather than it is that of God. In a couple of instances, howbeit, its author used the Kingdom of God.

Why is that? What differentiates the two? The Lord taught the Kingdom of God, of His Father, which is the only one in heaven: love. Inasmuch that Luke, Mark, and John use only such wording. Using another one brings only confusion in one's mind. Yet again, it's apparent this record is copied from Luke and Mark, and this only adds to the long list of its manifold incoherencies.

It's the first book, the story starting the New Testament. It opens God's Good News Stories list. Why? What's the goal of such order? Why wasn't it until now challenged by the authorities of the Bible's various versions? It seems evident the purpose of this book is to create doubts and lead astray. Making it the first in the New Testament is purposed to present it as the reference of Jesus' story for any new reader. However, with so many errors, it can't be an oversight, but willfully intended to subtly mislead and remove the trust one may have in God by making the three subsequent stories look inaccurate and, consequently, all God's teachings. John's first letter in 4:1–3 reminds not to trust every spirit: *"Beloved, do not believe every spirit, but test the spirits, whether they are of God; because many false prophets have gone out into the world. By this you know the Spirit of God: Every spirit that confesses that Jesus Christ has come in the flesh is of God, and every spirit that does not confess that Jesus Christ has come in the flesh is not of God. And this is the spirit of the Antichrist, which you have heard was coming, and is now already in the world."* (NKJV)

Making it the first record of the Lord Jesus' ministry de facto makes it, unconsciously, the reference of them all. Therefore, believing those remaining who recount the truth becomes tedious and cumbersome; it seems incoherent and doubtful. Thus, one has trouble believing in the Word as a whole. What this story does is to teach a lie as being the truth, to make people doubt when they're facing the reality. Such craftiness is simply devilish. No wonder all debates make use of these incoherencies and movies often use that story. Indeed, many will place such at the forefront of their debates against

God's existence. This is a Trojan horse placed in the Bible to discredit God's Way of salvation in Jesus Christ. It shows how crafty means are in this battle against the ruling powers in the heavenly realm, and the obedience of the very ones who are supposed to stand for the Good News of God.

5.   Many apostles have often restated teachers of the Good News will be judged more severely, as reads James 3:1, "*My brethren, let not many of you become teachers, knowing that we shall receive a stricter judgment.*" (NKJV)

Moreover, the book of Revelation in verses 22:18–19 gives a more serious warning than what's said in the story of Matthew: "*. . . If anyone adds to these things, God will add to him the plagues that are written in this book; and if anyone takes away from the words of the book of this prophecy, God shall take away his part from the Book of Life, from the holy city, and from the things which are written in this book.*" (NKJV)

However, Matthew instead says in 5:19, "*Whoever therefore breaks one of the least of these commandments, and teaches men so, shall be called least in the kingdom of heaven; . . .*" (NKJV)

Rebelling against God's commandments won't allow entrance into the Kingdom of God, but rather will lead to eternal death in the lake of fire and brimstone. Nothing defiled will ever enter Zion, the Holy city of God. It's written in Revelation 21:27, "*. . . there shall by no means enter it anything that defiles, or causes an abomination or a lie, but only those who are written in the Lamb's Book of Life.*" (NKJV)

6.   Paul and Luke use the word fool, but Matthew states such linguistic is worth to be in hellfire, as verse 5:22 reads, "*But I say to you that whoever is angry with his brother without a cause shall be in danger of the judgment. And whoever says to his brother, 'Raca!' shall be in danger of the council. But whoever says, 'You fool!' shall be in danger of hell fire.*" (NKJV)

Yet this word, used many times in the Bible's various books, especially in Proverbs and Ecclesiastes, has been used by God in a parable. What are the implications? Does it apply to the Lord's case? Will God contradict Himself? He is the One Who never lies; He's Holy! From His mouth, truth manifests a Wisdom that has no limit, thus is infinite. As Luke's parable in 12:16–21 reads, *"Then He spoke a parable to them, saying: 'The ground of a certain rich man yielded plentifully. And he thought within himself, saying, "What shall I do, since I have no room to store my crops?" So he said, "I will do this: I will pull down my barns and build greater, and there I will store all my crops and my goods. And I will say to my soul, 'Soul, you have many goods laid up for many years; take your ease; eat, drink, and be merry.'" But God said to him, "Fool! This night your soul will be required of you; then whose will those things be which you have provided?" So is he who lays up treasure for himself, and is not rich toward God.'"* (NKJV)

The apostle Paul, in his first address to the Corinthians, uses that expression in 15:35–36. *"But someone will ask, 'How are the dead raised? What kind of body will they have when they come back?" You fool! The seed you plant does not come to life unless it dies,"* (ISV)

Luke's experience of the ministry is from being the apostle Paul's doctor and closest friend during his ministry. Paul's ministry was recognized by the apostles Peter, John, and James, perceived themselves as columns of the Good News of Jesus Christ, as attested by the letter sent to the Galatians in 2:9. *"and when they perceived the grace that was given unto me, James and Cephas and John, they who were reputed to be pillars, gave to me and Barnabas the right hands of fellowship, that we should go unto the Gentiles, and they unto the circumcision,"* (ERV)

He received his ministry by a revelation from the Lord, as he declared it to the Galatians in 1:11–12. *"But I make known to you, brethren, that the gospel which was preached by me is not according to man. For I neither received it from man, nor was I taught it, but it came through the revelation of Jesus Christ."* (NKJV)

The apostle Peter on the apostle Paul writes in his second letter in 3:15–16. *"and consider that the longsuffering of our Lord is salvation—as also our beloved brother Paul, according to the wisdom given to him, has written to you, as also in all his epistles, speaking in them of these things, in which are some things hard to understand, which untaught and unstable people twist to their own destruction, as they do also the rest of the Scriptures."* (NKJV)

7.   The apostle John instructs not to salute one that denies Christ's earthly existence; however, Matthew's story teaches the opposite in 5:47. *"And if you greet your brethren only, what do you do more than others? Do not even the tax collectors do so?"* (NKJV)

More appropriate, therefore, is the word sent by the apostle John in his second letter that reads in verses 1:7–11, *"For many deceivers have gone out into the world who do not confess Jesus Christ as coming in the flesh. This is a deceiver and an antichrist. Look to yourselves, that we do not lose those things we worked for, but that we may receive a full reward. Whoever transgresses and does not abide in the doctrine of Christ does not have God. He who abides in the doctrine of Christ has both the Father and the Son. If anyone comes to you and does not bring this doctrine, do not receive him into your house nor greet him; for he who greets him shares in his evil deeds."* (NKJV)

With all these deliberate inaccuracies, skillfully designed to target the foundation of the Good News guidelines, isn't it the author of the Matthew record found likewise in that saying? *"many deceivers have gone out into the world who do not confess Jesus Christ as coming in the flesh. This is a deceiver and an antichrist."* (NKJV)

8.   The Lord took our infirmities on the cross, and thereby made a spectacle of the insurgents in the heavenly realm, as written in Colossians 2:14–15. *"Having wiped out the handwriting of requirements that was against us, which was contrary to us. And He has taken it out of the way, having nailed it to the cross. Having disarmed principalities and powers, He made a public spectacle of them, triumphing over them in it."* (NKJV)

In the Matthew story, however, a rather different viewpoint is given of what was the atonement as reads verses 8:16-17.

"That evening they brought to him many who were oppressed by demons, and he cast out the spirits with a word and healed all who were sick. This was to fulfill what was spoken by the prophet Isaiah: 'He took our illnesses and bore our diseases.'" (ESV)

The author of the Matthew story used this quote out of its right context, as if while ministering, Christ took up our sins. Surely, He destroyed the works of the devil by healing the diseases. However, it's on the cross that all was accomplished, as established in Isaiah's prophecy 53:4-5. *"Surely he has borne our griefs and carried our sorrows; yet we esteemed him stricken, smitten by God, and afflicted. But he was pierced for our transgressions; he was crushed for our iniquities; upon him was the chastisement that brought us peace, and with his wounds we are healed."* (ESV)

Though this seems negligible, it fosters confusion in one's mind, even contradicting what the apostle Paul confirmed in explaining that principle by saying in 1 Corinthians 2:7–8, *"But we impart a secret and hidden wisdom of God, which God decreed before the ages for our glory. None of the rulers of this age understood this, for if they had, they would not have crucified the Lord of glory."* (ESV)

If the evil forces in heavenly realms who orchestrated the crucifixion of the Lord, even the fallen angels knew what the Church teaches now, they would've realized the Lord's assassination wouldn't help their purpose. The cross having wiped out all sins, those who walk as the Lord commanded can no longer be accused by the devil before God the Father, for they no longer have sins: they are therefore called saints, as the apostle Paul says in the introduction to his letter to the Colossians in 1:1-2. *"Paul, an apostle of Jesus Christ by the will of God, and Timothy our brother, To the saints and faithful brethren in Christ who are in Colosse."* (NKJV)

9. In some scriptures, the author of Matthew uses a double instance without meaningful nor coherent belief supporting these facts: From the two blind men who recovered sight, of which Mark, author of his chronicle's source, identified with a

name and surname, as 10:46 reads, *"Now they came to Jericho. As He went out of Jericho with His disciples and a great multitude, blind Bartimaeus, the son of Timaeus, sat by the road begging."* (NKJV)

If Mark clearly identified the beggar with a name and surname, why is that Matthew's author doubles that instance, like he did also with the donkey on which the Lord entered in Jerusalem? No logical reasoning upholds such language: Did the Lord stand with a foot on each donkey? Numerous indeed are those trying to make God's Word look like a circus, yet their reward doesn't sleep. Because the Matthew account reads in 20:29–30, *"Now as they went out of Jericho, a great multitude followed Him. And behold, two blind men sitting by the road, when they heard that Jesus was passing by, cried out, saying, "Have mercy on us, O Lord, Son of David!"* (NKJV)

Why pervert the original record with these ambiguous interpretations, other than to lead many astray? Zechariah's oracle in 9:9 reads, *"Rejoice greatly, O daughter of Zion! Shout, O daughter of Jerusalem! Behold, your King is coming to you; He is just and having salvation, Lowly and riding on a donkey, A colt, the foal of a donkey."* (NKJV)

Though many Bible versions contain that oddness in their translation, some newer ones have rectified it. Which leads us to inquire, what makes today a valid and accurate version of the Bible? Matthew's author has made his story more confusing than anything else, driving right minds away from the truth and, thus, from the faith.

10. The Son of man, even the Messiah which implies God coming in the midst of mankind as a mere human was that only One person able to forgive sins, which He afterward allowed His disciples to accomplish, as it's written in John 20:22–23. *"And when he had said this, he breathed on them and said to them, 'Receive the Holy Spirit. If you forgive the sins of any, they are forgiven them; if you withhold forgiveness from any, it is withheld."* (ESV)

It's through God's Holy Spirit those who are faithful can

intercede to have others' sins forgiven. Therefore, the apostle Paul urges people to bless, hence forbids them to curse because these actions are extremely great in magnitude. Christians are called to save souls from damnation, not add them to the list of Sheol: There are too many already. The multitude of false ministers, who are sorcerers and consequently have nothing to do with the Lord Jesus, aren't able to do such a thing because they don't have the Holy Spirit of God. Thus, they pray to devils, not Christ.

But once again, the author of Matthew bent the context by making believe any man is able to accomplish the forgiveness of sins. Matthew 9:8 reads, *"Now when the multitudes saw it, they marveled and glorified God, who had given such power to men."* (NKJV)

11. The author of Matthew recounts the Lord's miracles in such a way as to diminish the faith of the reader. We often act out of faith in our daily lives without realizing it. When one presses the button on the remote control to turn on the television, that's faith. Having the certainty that the equipment will turn on without the control being physically connected to it. If we imagine people in the sixties with their first television, they would never have imagined that this could be possible. In the same way, God raises our faith and tells us to ask and it will be given to us; knock and it will be opened; seek and we'll find. When the sick woman approached the Lord, the plight of her situation left no room for hesitation: She had to be healed, for she had tried everything and only got worse. As a last resort, she was even prepared to steal power from the Lord in order to be healed. So, she went and touched His garment, convinced that He was Holy (which is true), and that He was so powerful that touching the edge of His garment would be enough to cleanse her of this affliction (which is also true), so that's how she proceeded. Notice that just like the television, the assumptions must be true for the miracle to manifest. There is an inscription on the remote control that tells you

where to press to turn on the television. If you believe what's written and press the button, having followed the instructions, you will get the expected result. It's the same with the power of the Lord: He said to ask according to His will and we will receive if we believe it is so. Surely, we cannot waver in our faith or ask for evil and expect Him to grant our request. Our demand must be made out of love, and we must believe that He, as the Almighty God in heaven and our loving Father, is able to grant it. If we are confident in our devices, knowing that engineers paid by established companies have worked diligently to make them possible, how much more should our faith be in the Lord, knowing that He is Almighty, the author of all existence in the whole of creation, who exercises justice and steadfast love toward His children.

In Matthew's story, however, the author minimizes the woman's actions, which is a way of preventing readers from imitating what she did. Nevertheless, in other accounts, it's clear that many have successfully followed this path, as we read in Mark 6:56 *"And wherever he came, in villages, cities, or countryside, they laid the sick in the marketplaces and implored him that they might touch even the fringe of his garment. And as many as touched it were made well."* (ESV)

But a different version of events is recounted in Matthew 9:22, which explains that, *"Jesus turned, and seeing her he said, "Take heart, daughter; your faith has made you well." And instantly the woman was made well."* (ESV)

Take note, it's not when the Lord turned to her that she was healed, but when she touched the fringe of His garment, as this is what prone the Lord to inquire who had touched Him, as written in Mark 5:25–29. *"And there was a woman who had had a discharge of blood for twelve years, and who had suffered much under many physicians, and had spent all that she had, and was no better but rather grew worse. She had heard the reports about Jesus and came up behind him in the crowd and touched his garment. For she said, "If I touch even his garments, I will be made well." And immediately the flow of blood dried up, and she felt in her body that she was healed of her disease.”* (ESV)

We can see from this first part of that story, the woman had heard about Jesus' testimony and was convinced He was the Son of God and a Holy man, inasmuch that touching only the fringe of His garment would restore her health. That's faith—the certainty that something is true—and the action follows what is thought. The result is consequently manifested through such an act on her part. Take note: She didn't ask the Lord if she could do such a thing, but just touched His clothes. Also, many others were touching Him, which shows her faith is what manifested the miracle.

Mark 55:30–34 illustrates the surprise of the Lord and the disposition of that woman's heart. Surely, as a Pharisee, He would have been offended to have been touched by an unclean person—a flux of blood from a woman being depicted as such by the law of Moses. As such, she feared retaliation on His part. Notice that she appeared amid the crowd from behind, expecting to go unnoticed. But the Holy Spirit of God is truth, thus revealing all things. And moreover, in her situation, she needed to know she couldn't steal anything from the Lord because He is Merciful and Compassionate, which means He delights in doing good and saving His people. As such, when prophesying about the Lord's truthful compassion, Isaiah said the following in verses 55:1–2, *“Come, everyone who thirsts, come to the waters; and he who has no money, come, buy and eat! Come, buy wine and milk without money and without price. Why do you spend your money for that which is not bread, and your labor for that which does not satisfy? Listen diligently to me, and eat what is good, and delight yourselves in rich food.”* (ESV)

Thus, she needed to know the difference between the Lord's stance and the Pharisees. And, as the prophet Jeremiah said in 9:24, *“let him who boasts boast in this, that he understands and knows me, that I am the Lord who practices steadfast love, justice, and righteousness in the earth. For in these things I delight, declares the Lord.”*

(ESV)

So, her faith healed her and the Lord felt power leaving Him. He turned to see who had such strong faith. Mark 5:30–34 reads, *"And Jesus, perceiving in himself that power had gone out from him, immediately turned about in the crowd and said, 'Who touched my garments?' And his disciples said to him, 'You see the crowd pressing around you, and yet you say, 'Who touched me?'' And he looked around to see who had done it. But the woman, knowing what had happened to her, came in fear and trembling and fell down before him and told him the whole truth. And he said to her, 'Daughter, your faith has made you well; go in peace, and be healed of your disease.'"* (ESV)

12. Mark's and Luke's reports communicate the Pharisees' blasphemy against the Holy Spirit, with the Lord's reaction clarifying why this can't be true. But Matthew's author left this to the reader's interpretation. No explanation is provided, though it's clearly mentioned in Mark's and Luke's reports, sources of his account. Instead, his story progresses to the next topic. Matthew reads in verses 9:32–35, *"As they were going away, behold, a demon-oppressed man who was mute was brought to him. And when the demon had been cast out, the mute man spoke. And the crowds marveled, saying, 'Never was anything like this seen in Israel.' But the Pharisees said, 'He casts out demons by the prince of demons.' And Jesus went throughout all the cities and villages, teaching in their synagogues and proclaiming the gospel of the kingdom and healing every disease and every affliction."* (ESV)

We can perceive the cunningness of this scheme, which firstly instills many wrong perceptions of the Lord's ministry, with false and misleading ideas, then removes convincing arguments to weaken the truth even more, letting doubt and erroneous conceptions flourish. It gives the impression the Lord either acquiesced with their denunciations or had no response to such an accusation, which is very far from what happened. It is written in Mark 3:22–30, *"And the scribes who came down from Jerusalem were saying, 'He is possessed by Beelzebul,'" and "by the prince of demons he casts out the demons." And he called them to him and said to them in parables, "How can Satan cast out Satan? If a kingdom is divided against itself, that kingdom cannot stand. And if a house is divided against itself, that house will not be able to stand. And if Satan has risen up against himself and is divided, he cannot stand, but is coming to an end. But no one can enter a strong man's house and plunder his goods, unless he first binds the strong man. Then indeed he may plunder his house. "Truly, I say to you, all sins will be forgiven the children of man, and whatever blasphemies they utter, but whoever blasphemes against the Holy Spirit never has forgiveness, but is guilty of an eternal sin—for they were saying, 'He has an unclean spirit.'"* (ESV)

Likewise, Luke's account relates in verses 11:14–20 an important truth about what was said: His accusers were in fact those they alleged He was, proving their allegiance. *"Now he was casting out a demon that was mute. When the demon had gone out, the mute man spoke, and the people marveled. But some of them said, "He casts out demons by Beelzebul, the prince of demons," while others, to test him, kept seeking from him a sign from heaven. But he, knowing their thoughts, said to them, "Every kingdom divided against itself is laid waste, and a divided household falls. And if Satan also is divided against himself, how will his kingdom stand? For you say that I cast out demons by Beelzebul. And if I cast out demons by Beelzebul, by whom do your sons cast them out? Therefore they will be your judges. But if it is by the finger of God that I cast out demons, then the kingdom of God has come upon you."* (ESV)

Notice that to allege the Lord has an unclean spirit is an attempt to make God look like the devil and vice versa.

13. Serpents have a clear connotation in the whole Bible that they represent the devil, and no good example is given about them: they symbolize what's evil, as described in Revelation 20:2. *"And he seized the dragon, that ancient serpent, who is the devil and Satan, and bound him for a thousand years,"* (ESV)

The two exceptions to that rule are when the serpent is used by Aaron against Pharaoh's sorcerers, and yet it's not something one would try to do. It was an illustration of God's power above men's various enchantments, even those numerous sorcerers around Pharaoh. The other one is when Moses makes the image of a serpent, which he asked the Israelites to look upon when they were bitten by serpents in the desert, showing thereby what Christians will experience when looking at the cross of Jesus Christ. Hence, it clarifies why the Lord said to Nicodemus in John 3:14–15, *"And as Moses lifted up the serpent in the wilderness, so must the Son of Man be lifted up, that whoever believes in him may have eternal life."* (ESV) Like to the Pharisees, as reads John 8:28, *"So Jesus said to them, "When you have lifted up the Son of Man, then you will know that I am he, and that I do nothing on my own authority, but speak just as the Father taught me."* (ESV)

The Matthew story is the only place a serpent's illustration is presented with a positive meaning to imitate. It advises disciples to be prudent like serpents, which clearly is made to foster that confusion pattern that started at the beginning. Nowhere else is it advised to do anything like a serpent, yet Matthew 10:16 states, *"Behold, I am sending you out as sheep in the midst of wolves, so be wise as serpents and innocent as doves."* (ESV)

Since when is the serpent considered wise in the whole Bible? Isn't it the expression of the rebellion of the devil, the leader and father of lies that bring hatred, seen as ignorance? How can ignorance be wisdom?

14. Matthew is the only record that teaches to flee from city to city, as verse 10:23 reads, *"When they persecute you in this city, flee to another. For assuredly, I say to you, you will not have gone through the cities of Israel before the Son of Man comes."* (NKJV)

Not only does it contradict faith's action with patience through the Peace received from the Holy Spirit, but the last part of the scripture today proves to be a false prophecy: Judah was destroyed and disciples had been through all its cities to preach, and the Lord is yet to come. Nowhere else is such falsity found in the Bible. On the contrary, believers oftentimes are asked to patiently bear the reproach, as Job did, because God is above all the creation and He's the One that allows it. In particular, this can be seen in Revelation 2:10. *"Do not fear what you are about to suffer. Behold, the devil is about to throw some of you into prison, that you may be tested, and for ten days you will have tribulation. Be faithful unto death, and I will give you the crown of life."* (ESV)

The Lord allows His children to be tested by all the devil's maneuvers, to strengthen their faith, as was the case for Job. Just as students have exams and surprise quizzes, so Christians have tribulations to validate and demonstrate how they have progressed in that firm assurance for the Lord.

On the other hand, if evildoers are to this day not yet judged, isn't it because God demonstrates His patience? Allowing time to repent before judgment day? The apostle Paul in his first address to the Thessalonians exhorts as it's written in 3:3, *". . . no one should be shaken by these afflictions; for you yourselves know that we are appointed to this."* (NKJV) Likewise, in his second letter to the Corinthians explaining his ministry in 6:4, he wrote, *"But in all things we commend ourselves as ministers of God: in much patience, in tribulations, in needs, in distresses,"* (NKJV)

Yet again, in that same letter, he wrote in 12:12, *"The signs of a true apostle were performed among you with utmost patience, with signs and wonders and mighty works."* (ESV)

His prayer for the Colossians was per 1:11, which says, *"being strengthened with all power, according to his glorious might, for all endurance and patience with joy,"* (ESV)

The comforting apostle Peter reminds in his first letter that reads in verse 3:14, *"But even if you should suffer for righteousness' sake, you are blessed. "And do not be afraid of their threats, nor be troubled."* (NKJV)

Likewise, James in the start of his exhortation tells in verse 1:12, *"Blessed is the man who endures temptation; for when he has been approved, he will receive the crown of life which the Lord has promised to those who love Him."* (NKJV) Continuing in verses 5:10–11, he admonishes in a like manner, *"My brethren, take the prophets, who spoke in the name of the Lord, as an example of suffering and patience. Indeed we count them blessed who endure. You have heard of the perseverance of Job and seen the end intended by the Lord—that the Lord is very compassionate and merciful."* (NKJV)

In three instances, a man of God tried to flee to a different city. All were prophets. Uriah, as reported Jeremiah 26:21–23. *"And when King Jehoiakim, with all his warriors and all the officials, heard his words, the king sought to put him to death. But when Uriah heard of it, he was afraid and fled and escaped to Egypt. Then King Jehoiakim sent to Egypt certain men, Elnathan the son of Achbor and others with him, and they took Uriah from Egypt and brought him to King Jehoiakim, who struck him down with the sword and dumped his dead body into the burial place of the common people."* (ESV)

Likewise, Jeremiah also tried to flee to Benjamin, as Jeremiah 37:11–15 reads, *"And it happened, when the army of the Chaldeans left the siege of Jerusalem for fear of Pharaoh's army, that Jeremiah went out of Jerusalem to go into the land of Benjamin to claim his property there among the people. And when he was in the Gate of Benjamin, a captain of the guard was there whose name was Irijah the son of Shelemiah, the son of Hananiah; and he seized Jeremiah the prophet, saying, "You are defecting to the Chaldeans!" Then Jeremiah said, "False! I am not defecting to the Chaldeans." But he did not listen to him. So Irijah seized Jeremiah and brought him to the princes. Therefore the princes were angry with Jeremiah, and they struck him and put him in prison in the house of Jonathan the scribe. For they had made that the prison."* (NKJV)

The most publicized is Jonah trying to go to Tarshish because he didn't want to prophesy at Nineveh, as he was seeking God's Wrath to come upon that wicked kingdom. In all these cases, Uriah's death, Jeremiah's imprisonment, and Jonah being swallowed by a big fish are all taught in a principle the apostle Paul elucidated with his first letter to the Corinthians in verse 11:32. *"But when we are judged, we are*

chastened by the Lord, that we may not be condemned with the world."
(NKJV)

Note that Uriah's punishment is probably more severe because he broke a command of the Lord: "Find help under the shadow of Egypt," repeatedly forbidden. We're chastised by the Lord since we're examples, and our wrongs can cause much more prejudices in others' lives, as prophesied by Ezekiel in 33:12. ". . . *The righteousness of the righteous shall not deliver him when he transgresses . . .*" (ESV)

A car driving slowly can maneuver easily and avoid obstacles without harm, unlike one that is speeding. Likewise, we have that much responsibility as being ambassadors of the Holy Kingdom of God. We, and more so God, cannot tolerate our wrong behavior. We are therefore chastised to avoid further mistakes, as Luke reported in 12:48. "*Everyone to whom much was given, of him much will be required, and from him to whom they entrusted much, they will demand the more.*" (ESV)

One may say, isn't it Elijah and Jesus fled for their lives? The Lord withdrew to Ephraim, for His appointed time wasn't set yet. Wherefore, to avoid being killed before the Passover, He stayed in that country by the wilderness. Elijah, on the other hand, took his servant in a different city for that one's safety, yet himself left for the wilderness, requesting that God kill him. Thus, he did not seek safety as it reads in 1 Kings 19:3. "*And when he saw that, he arose and ran for his life, and went to Beersheba, which belongs to Judah, and left his servant there. But he himself went a day's journey into the wilderness, and came and sat down under a broom tree. And he prayed that he might die, and said, 'It is enough! Now, Lord, take my life, for I am no better than my fathers!'*"
(NKJV)

The Lord in Revelation shows how He considers the believer who is patient, as 3:10 reads, "*Because you have kept my word about patient endurance, I will keep you from the hour of trial that is coming on the whole world, to try those who dwell on the earth.*" (ESV)

The teachings in Matthew in no way advocate the biblical

principles of truth, so they are not of the Holy Spirit.

15. Tweaking expressions is surely the art upheld by cunning liars. Changing wordings to give a different and rather distorted view is what the Matthew story does, as verse 10:35 declares, *"For I have come to set a man against his father, and a daughter against her mother, and a daughter-in-law against her mother-in- law."* (ESV)

The apostle Paul teaches what it's like to be carnal-minded, or to live per this world and the teachings of the devil, in Titus 3:3. *". . . foolish, disobedient, deceived, serving various lusts and pleasures, living in malice and envy, hateful and hating one another."* (NKJV)

How could God have love as His intrinsic nature and yet come as a man on earth to bring quarrels between His children? Then lay down His life to bear all of mankind's sins on the cross for atonement? All that is illogical. Isn't that story's writer insidiously yet steadily trying to make readers believe Holy is evil and bad is good? In Mark 9:50, the Lord clearly recommended one of the Holy Spirit's fruits: *". . . be at peace with one another."* (ESV)

God is of peace and truth, and the Lord has said to have come for a judgment, as reads John 9:39. *"Jesus said, 'For judgment I came into this world, that those who do not see may see, and those who see may become blind.'"* (ESV)

If indeed, a division is set on earth, it's because those of God will separate themselves from the devil's sons and not because God wants chaos to be started on earth. Luke 12:51–53 reads, *"Do you think that I have come to give peace on earth? No, I tell you, but rather division. For from now on in one house there will be five divided, three against two and two against three. They will be divided, father against son and son against father, mother against daughter and daughter against mother, mother-in-law against her daughter-in-law and daughter-in- law against mother-in-law."* (ESV)

It's evident both versions relate a totally different perspective of what's done. Yet because Matthew is placed as the first story in the New Testament, it gives the unconscious conviction it is the reference of the plain truth. Howbeit, being a falsity, it makes the subsequent to seem unfitting and rather awkward. Teaching lies as the truth started in Eden and is still applied nowadays. Unfortunately, it has a certain success with people who are unaware. We separate ourselves from evil ones by confessing the Lord Jesus Christ and applying His love principles, in spite of the fierce persecution set to dismantle our faith in an attempt to corrupt our mind and conduct. And regardless of these subsequent consequences, we are called to live in peace with all the people around us. This is explained in 1 Peter 2:12. *"Keep your conduct among the Gentiles honorable, so that when they speak against you as evildoers, they may see your good deeds and glorify God on the day of visitation."* (ESV)

16. It's certain that a little lie here and there can't be spotted right away, yet they still add up and cause confusion. The Lord often spoke about both aspects of our existence: spiritual and physical. Attempting to save the physical life causes the loss of the spiritual one, even life eternal. It is the reason why the Lord explained in Mark 8:35–38 what the principles are in upholding our life on earth to make it a success and access the Holy Kingdom. *"For whoever would save his life will lose it, but whoever loses his life for my sake and the gospel's will save it. For what does it profit a man to gain the whole world and forfeit his soul? For what can a man give in return for his soul? For whoever is ashamed of me and of my words in this adulterous and sinful generation, of him will the Son of Man also be ashamed when he comes in the glory of his Father with the holy angels."* (ESV)

This is not a pledge for poverty and laziness, but the admonition that confessing the Lord and applying His teachings will set one apart and stir up outrage from the world. Thus, such one will be thoroughly persecuted.

However, in the story named Matthew, the author affirmation gives the impression that any one success in life isn't matching God's standard in 10:39. *"Whoever finds his life will lose it, and whoever loses his life for my sake will find it."* (ESV)

Men of God in the past have been successful—even wealthy—and honorable. Examples include Job, Abraham, Isaac, Jacob, Joseph, David, and especially Solomon. Living for this world is what makes the whole unfitting. If we use the world, we are not from there and shouldn't act as such, with all its lust and various perversions.

17. Estimating a crowd is hard enough, let alone having to distinguish genders and generations. Mankind simply has no such ability, especially for large crowds. Nevertheless, the author of Matthew relates when the Lord multiplied bread and fish for the multitudes, such were five thousand, without woman and children. Either a crowd comprises a mix of persons who can't be differentiated or it is only made of one gender, which allows to define it as such. In the case of the Lord, people came from villages and cities with their sick ones who could have been of any gender and age. Such affirmation is one more fallacy that adds doubt in the minds of readers who will question how this numbering was accomplished. Hence, Mark and Luke only give the number of people in the crowd without specifying its composition. Since both books are templates used by Matthew's author, why did he add such misleading information, other than to create the skepticism about that story's authenticity? It's written in Matthew 14:21, *"And those who ate were about five thousand men, besides women and children."* (ESV) Similarly, it's again stated in verse 15:38. *"Those who ate were four thousand men, besides women and children."* (ESV)

18. Christ's actions of casting demons by His word, calming the sea's rage, raising dead people, and healing the sick are all an illustration of God coming in the flesh as the Messiah and portray His complete Sovereignty over the whole creation. Believers who will later follow His teachings and walk in His

footsteps will likewise overcome the world by their faith, even all the devil's lies. Consequently, the apostle John depicts them in Revelation 15:2. *"And I saw something like a sea of glass mingled with fire, and those who have the victory over the beast, over his image and over his mark and over the number of his name, standing on the sea of glass, having harps of God."* (NKJV)

Water often represents the spiritual world, and the sea is the abode of the leviathan, an illustration of the devil, as Isaiah describes in 27:1. *"In that day the LORD with his hard and great and strong sword will punish Leviathan the fleeing serpent, Leviathan the twisting serpent, and he will slay the dragon that is in the sea."* (ESV)

Therefore, the Lord Jesus walking on water has a meaning of superiority. Besides, water is another image of manifold races of different kinds of people, as reads Revelation 17:15. *"And the angel said to me, "The waters that you saw, where the prostitute is seated, are peoples and multitudes and nations and languages."* (ESV)

When the author of Matthew says Peter walked on water with Jesus, it doesn't align with the Lord's teachings: Peter was converted when he received the Holy Spirit, not before. Thus, he hadn't conquered this world by his faith, as the apostle John explains in verses 5:4–5 of his first letter who is the overcomer of this world. *"For everyone who has been born of God overcomes the world. And this is the victory that has overcome the world—our faith. Who is it that overcomes the world except the one who believes that Jesus is the Son of God?"* (ESV)

Howbeit, the night He was betrayed, the Lord told Peter to strengthen his brethren once converted, meaning that up to that point he hadn't been, since the Holy Spirit hasn't been sent to them; the Lord would send it during the Pentecost. Luke 22:31–32 says, *"Simon, Simon, behold, Satan demanded to have you, that he might sift you like wheat, but I have prayed for you that your faith may not fail. And when you have turned again, strengthen your brothers."* (ESV)

Peter denying the Lord is the evidence he wasn't yet converted, thus couldn't overcome the world as shown.

Matthew's author, however, tells otherwise in 14:28. *"And Peter answered him, 'Lord, if it is you, command me to come to you on the water.' He said, 'Come.' So Peter got out of the boat and walked on the water and came to Jesus. But when he saw the wind, he was afraid, and beginning to sink he cried out, 'Lord, save me.' Jesus immediately reached out his hand and took hold of him, saying to him, 'O you of little faith, why did you doubt?'"* (ESV)

Once again, this section was added to the original version, only to mislead and raise suspicion in one's heart.

19. We are all liable if we ever forsake God's orders, with no exception. The apostle Peter states that reality in reproving people's misbehaves in the Church in 2 Peter 2:20–21. *"For if, after they have escaped the defilements of the world through the knowledge of our Lord and Savior Jesus Christ, they are again entangled in them and overcome, the last state has become worse for them than the first. For it would have been better for them never to have known the way of righteousness than after knowing it to turn back from the holy commandment delivered to them."* (ESV)

Stating the doors of hell will not prevail against the Church gives the impression that people, once they were within the Church, were allowed to do whatever they wished without consequence, which is completely wrong. God is Holy and does not make exception for anyone. On the contrary, He will chastise those of His disciples who go astray, to prevent death eternal.

Matthew 16:17–19 reads, "And Jesus answered him, *"Blessed are you, Simon Bar-Jonah! For flesh and blood has not revealed this to you, but my Father who is in heaven. And I tell you, you are Peter, and on this rock I will build my church, and the gates of hell shall not prevail against it. I will give you the keys of the kingdom of heaven, and whatever you bind on earth shall be bound in heaven, and whatever you loose on earth shall be loosed in heaven."* (ESV)

This declaration made only by the author of Matthew about Peter being the foundation upon which the Church will be built is once again questionable. The Holy city's wall in Heaven has the twelve apostles' names as its foundation, not only the apostle Peter (Revelation 21:14). Moreover, when God testifies the Lord Jesus is indeed His Son on the mountain, Peter is with John and James, as reads Mark 9:2. The apostle reiterated it in his letter in 2 Peter 1:17–18. *"For when he received honor and glory from God the Father, and the voice was borne to him by the Majestic Glory, 'This is my beloved Son, with whom I am well pleased,' we ourselves heard this very voice borne from heaven, for we were with him on the holy mountain."* (ESV)

After His resurrection, the Lord breathed on all the reunited disciples, except Judas Iscariot and Thomas, who doubted the resurrection. Thus, ten apostles and probably other disciples were present and received that blessing, which will be manifested for many more on the day of Pentecost. Therefore, Peter is not the only one who will be able to hold or forgive sins, despite what the wording of Matthew's story entices to believe, as it's written in John 20:22–23. *"And when he had said this, he breathed on them and said to them, 'Receive the Holy Spirit. If you forgive the sins of any, they are forgiven them; if you withhold forgiveness from any, it is withheld.'"* (ESV)

20. The Lord lived on the donations from people, as mentioned, for example, in Luke 8:3. *"and Joanna, the wife of Chuza, Herod's household manager, and Susanna, and many others, who provided for them out of their means."* (ESV)

He could have lived a fancy life without the sufferings of this world, but that wasn't the case. Such would have made God's law a covering of hypocrisy, which it isn't. God is Holy and makes no exception, not even for the Savior. Thus, He suffered afflictions, just as any other human on earth. When sitting tired by the well in Sychar of Samaria, before the woman arrived, He could have had the water come out of it so he could drink. Rather, he waited for someone to give Him water. He was often invited in people's house, and when He was not,

He slept often outside, such as in the mount of olives, for example. Therefore, to have sent Peter fishing to get the money needed for tribute is inconsistent. When He cursed the fig tree on the way to Jerusalem from Bethany, He was hungry, meaning they had not eaten. Nor was it the case when Pharisees accused the disciples to pluck and eat heads of grain from the field they were crossing, which was prohibited by the law. All this only demonstrates He lived a life of a humble man, thus His ministry had very little and would've lived otherwise if the events in Matthew's story were true. As verse 17:27 reads, *"However, not to give offense to them, go to the sea and cast a hook and take the first that comes up, and when you open its mouth you will find a shekel. Take that and give it to them for me and for yourself."* (ESV)

Why did Peter have to go fishing? Why not find that money under a rock, as his name's meaning Cephas? Did he always walk with his boat on the shoulder? How long would it take to get the fish and the money then come back to pay? We can see all this is purely deceitful, making all of that story nothing but a hurting thorn in the reader's mind.

21. Children are open for instruction and believe what is said. Because they are innocent, they don't doubt what is taught to them; they see the world through the eyes of love. In that regard, so do Christians, who live by love's rules. The apostle Paul explained in his first letter to the Corinthians what it is to experience love, as written in verses 13:4–8. *"Love bears all things, believes all things, hopes all things, endures all things."* (ESV)

The Lord Jesus explained in Luke 22:26–27 how it looks to be a leader. *"… not so with you. Rather, let the greatest among you become as the youngest, and the leader as one who serves. For who is the greater, one who reclines at table or one who serves? Is it not the one who reclines at table? But I am among you as the one who serves."* (ESV)

Ministering to others is what makes one great in the Kingdom of God, which is love, not merely behaving like a child. Faith is alive when acts of kindness are done toward the ones in need. But Matthew's author teaches otherwise in 18:3–4. *"… "Truly, I say to you, unless you turn and become like children, you will never enter the kingdom of heaven. Whoever humbles himself like this child is the greatest in the kingdom of heaven."* (ESV)

Though it's subtle, the difference between the two is clear. Love is all about what goes on inside one's heart: Though we believe easily, it's with the knowledge of the truth and justice that we foster compassion and peace.

22. Does the teaching found in 18:15–17 promote peace and love within the Church? The apostle Paul said we must forgive and even tolerate when being wronged. It's written in 1 Corinthians 6:7. *"To have lawsuits at all with one another is already a defeat for you. Why not rather suffer wrong? Why not rather be defrauded?"* (ESV)

Love bears all things, endures all things, and does not insist on its own way. Mercy is what is always advised. One who sins deliberately, even after being warned, must be removed from the congregation. But if a difference of opinion is between two persons, counseling with patience must be the way to follow. Matthew reads in 18:15–17, *"If your brother sins against you, go and tell him his fault, between you and him alone. If he listens to you, you have gained your brother. But if he does not listen, take one or two others along with you, that every charge may be established by the evidence of two or three witnesses. If he refuses to listen to them, tell it to the church. And if he refuses to listen even to the church, let him be to you as a Gentile and a tax collector."* (ESV)

The next verse after this wrong teaching states the following in Matthew 18:18: *"Truly, I say to you, whatever you bind on earth shall be bound in heaven, and whatever you loose on earth shall be loosed in heaven."* (ESV)

Isn't it right there, in a very subtle way, an invitation to curse even brothers in the Church? The apostle Paul prohibited such in Romans 12:14, which reads, *"Bless those who persecute you; bless and do not curse them."* (ESV)

Besides, who are the two or three who must be called before reporting that matter to the Church? The apostle Paul teaches in 1 Corinthians 6:5–6, *"I say this to your shame. Can it be that there is no one among you wise enough to settle a dispute between the brothers, but brother goes to law against brother, and that before unbelievers?"* (ESV)

Christians must resolve their divergence between brothers, and not before unbelievers who don't have the Holy Spirit's wisdom to settle a matter. Consequently, in another letter, the apostle urges to resolve their matter and invites an elder to help them find a solution to their conflict. Undoubtably, there's a difference of opinion existing between these two believers, by the comment made in Philippians 4:2: *"I entreat Euodia and I entreat Syntyche to agree in the Lord. Yes, I ask you also, true companion, help these women, who have labored side by side with me in the gospel together with Clement and the rest of my fellow workers, whose names are in the book of life."* (ESV)

23. No one else teaches being with others will grant a prayer in the whole Bible. Such is according to God's plan and not the number of people assembled. It will certainly flag it as an urgent matter in heaven, just as fasting does, thus the apostle Paul, for example, urged believers to pray for them and people in positions of power. However, granting the plea is God's ruling. Also, believers need not to be many for their prayer to be heard in heaven, unlike Matthew 18:19-20. *"Again I say to you, if two of you agree on earth about anything they ask, it will be done for them by my Father in heaven. For where two or three are gathered in my name, there am I among them."* (ESV)

This even contradicts another rule in Matthew 6:5–6, when he advised to pray in secret. *"And when you pray, you must not be like the hypocrites. For they love to stand and pray in the synagogues and at the street corners, that they may be seen by others. Truly, I say to you, they have received their reward. But when you pray, go into your room and shut the door and pray to your Father who is in secret. And your Father who sees in secret will reward you."* (ESV)

Being two or three makes no difference, according to God's teachings, to the answering of a prayer. But keeping His commandments, which is obedience, is the act that changes everything, as the apostle Paul declares in 1 Corinthians 7:19. *"Circumcision is nothing and uncircumcision is nothing, but keeping the commandments of God is what matters."* (NKJV)

Walking in sanctification and, thus, in love makes a believer God's beloved one. Daniel's fasting and prayers for his people were done alone, like countless other petitions of the Lord's true servants. It's written in Daniel 9:23, *"At the beginning of your pleas for mercy a word went out, and I have come to tell it to you, for you are greatly loved. Therefore consider the word and understand the vision."* (ESV)

In the fish's belly, Jonah didn't expect anyone else to join him for his plea for mercy to be granted by God. Nor did Elijah pray with other people when, at his request, heaven didn't give rain for three years and six months; then when he prayed again, it poured down rain. Hence, intercession is successful when it's made by a righteous one, as James 5:16 says, *". . . The prayer of a righteous person has great power as it is working."* (NKJV)

Also, God is ever-present and abides in the heart of anyone who believes in Him, not because people assemble. Therefore, He is wherever any believer is, regardless of the amount of people around; the Holy Spirit abides in their hearts.

24. Uttering dark sayings that mean nothing and putting them in a book promoting wisdom is simply an expression of philosophy. What's the meaning behind forgiving seventy times sevenfold? Seventy is seven times ten. Ten is used as the number for a ruling to be established, and seven is used for God's implication. There are the ten judgments of Egypt, or the ten days of Daniel before serving Nebuchadnezzar in the royal court in Babylon, or the ten rulers who will precede

Armageddon and destroy Babylon, or the ten days of trials some will have before being appointed to the ministry by God, as written in Revelation 2:10. *"Do not fear what you are about to suffer. Behold, the devil is about to throw some of you into prison, that you may be tested, and for ten days you will have tribulation. Be faithful unto death, and I will give you the crown of life."* (ESV)

The seven days of the week or time of the creation to be as per God's plan, even seven heavenly days; the seven spirits before the Throne of God; Joseph is the seventh son of Jacob's wives; the death month of the prophet reversing God's orders and uttering false insights contradicting God's ones, in Jeremiah 28:16–17. *"Therefore thus says the Lord: 'Behold, I will remove you from the face of the earth. This year you shall die, because you have uttered rebellion against the Lord.'" In that same year, in the seventh month, the prophet Hananiah died."* (ESV)

Seventy was the number of people from Jacob who went to Egypt; there are the seventy weeks revealed in Daniel's prophecy for his people to be saved, and for seventy years, Israel was emptied of its inhabitants who were sent into exile in Babylon since they didn't honor God's Sabbaths as ordained, nor follow His orders, as reads 2 Chronicles 36:20–21. *"He took into exile in Babylon those who had escaped from the sword, and they became servants to him and to his sons until the establishment of the kingdom of Persia, to fulfill the word of the Lord by the mouth of Jeremiah, until the land had enjoyed its Sabbaths. All the days that it lay desolate it kept Sabbath, to fulfill seventy years."* (ESV)

There are several examples in the Bible that show a clear pattern with these numbers, some of which are less obvious than others. Like Adam's lifespan of nine hundred and thirty years, which show that he is seventy years short, or seven times ten to make a thousand years, or one heavenly day. So, as God declared in Genesis 2:17. *"... from the tree of the knowledge of good and evil you shall not eat, for on the day that you eat from it you will certainly die."* (NKJV)

And according to God's address, Adam died both spiritually

(instantly, for their eyes were opened), and physically (a heavenly day equivalent to a thousand years on earth), on the day of his transgression. Thus, proving the devil lied, even though it took many years to be revealed.

Nevertheless, seventy times seven remains the only one that is excluded from that outline. It doesn't mean anything per God's teachings and doctrines. Needless to say, this statement only appears in the story entitled Matthew.

25. The parable in Matthew 18:23–35 seems to give insight into God's law and ruling. However, there is a twist at the end making the whole thing a pure deceit. Does God change His ruling once it is established in the life of anyone? Such would have us live in continuous torment and fear of God's retaliation. It's written in Jeremiah 18:7–10, "*If at any time I declare concerning a nation or a kingdom, that I will pluck up and break down and destroy it, and if that nation, concerning which I have spoken, turns from its evil, I will relent of the disaster that I intended to do to it. And if at any time I declare concerning a nation or a kingdom that I will build and plant it, and if it does evil in my sight, not listening to my voice, then I will relent of the good that I had intended to do to it.*" (ESV) We can see from that scripture God intended to do something, but because of the behavior of his subjects, He changed His Word. But when a decision is made, will He come against what He has previously said? It's to perniciously state that God is not omniscient, that He would change a decision after He has ordained it because things didn't turn out the way He had intended. When He repented for the flood of Noah, a plan had already been established from the foundation of the world, thus the ark manifested that idea. He knows afore an existence how it will precisely manifest. There is nothing that surprised Him in all that happened within creation. He knew all before its origin. Otherwise, the world wouldn't have been created in seven days to allow Christ to come and save, then be perfected after three days, as He said to the Jews in Luke

13:32, when He will hand out the kingdom to His Father after having killed all His enemies. *"And He said to them, Go, tell that fox, 'Behold, I cast out demons and perform cures today and tomorrow, and the third day I shall be perfected.'"* (NKJV)

God often speaks afore time because He knows what lies ahead of us and warns us to allow for the success of our venture, as Jesus told the disciples in Mark 13:23, *"...be on guard; I have told you all things beforehand."* (ESV)

However, the parable in this case says God forgave, then changed the ruling because that person didn't do the same with his fellow. God knows the mischievous, and they're not stricken in this life, only to be found worthy of hell's fire. Wherefore, convinced nothing will ever happen to them, they behave wickedly till they face the reality of truth. Besides, wicked ones don't ask mercy of God. They can't communicate with Him because of their sins and have never proceeded in such manner, as it's written in Job 27:8–10. *"For what is the hope of the godless when God cuts him off, when God takes away his life? Will God hear his cry when distress comes upon him? Will he take delight in the Almighty? Will he call upon God at all times?"* (ESV)

Consequently, that parable is erroneous and misleading. God wants to save His people, those who love Him and respect His commandments. The reason why prophets speak aforetime is to prevent an irreversible situation. Therefore, it's wrong to say or let others believe God will forgive someone, then change His ruling to punish them due to future bad conduct. He searches our hearts, thus He knows our intentions even before we do. We move forward with God, and what we do in the present is what is being ruled. Thus, before it happens, we are warned to allow us to take the correct course of action when we're drifting. It's written in Ezekiel 18:21–28. *"if a wicked person turns away from all his sins that he has committed and keeps all my statutes and does what is just and right, he shall surely live; he shall not die. None of the transgressions that he has committed shall be remembered against him; for the righteousness that he has done he shall live. Have I any pleasure in the death of the wicked, declares the Lord God, and not rather that he should turn from his way and live? But when a righteous person turns away from his righteousness and does injustice and does the same abominations that the wicked person does, shall he live? None of the righteous deeds that he has done shall be remembered; for the treachery of which he is guilty and the sin he has committed, for them he shall die."* (ESV)

26. No other author says that one should divorce his wife because of sexual immorality, as Matthew 19:9 says. *"And I say to you, whoever divorces his wife, except for sexual immorality, and marries another, commits adultery; and whoever marries her who is divorced commits adultery."* (ESV)

In 1 Corinthians 7:11, the apostle Paul reiterates an order of the Lord: *"To the married I give this charge (not I, but the Lord): the wife should not separate from her husband (but if she does, she should remain unmarried or else be reconciled to her husband), and the husband should not divorce his wife."* (ESV)

The law of Moses, because of the hardness of the Israelites' hearts, permitted a certificate of divorce and the stoning of an adulterous woman, but the Lord Jesus overruled that matter, as the apostle Paul instructed. Which only confirms the ruling of the one caught in an act of adultery, as reported in John 8:10–11. *"Jesus stood up and said to her, 'Woman, where are they? Has no one condemned you?' She said, 'No one, Lord.' And Jesus said, 'Neither do I condemn you; go, and from now on sin no more.'"* (ESV)

This not only gives food for thought for anyone thinking about being married, as per the Lord, such contract can't be rescinded. But it also gives the opportunity to consider past examples like King David and Jacob. In both cases, their own sons defiled their marriage bed. Yet they didn't divorce their concubines. Rather, in the case of King David, and probably Jacob as well, they never approached them again. The Lord said through the prophecy of Jeremiah in 3:1, *"If a man divorces his wife and she goes from him and becomes another man's wife, will he return to her? Would not that land be greatly polluted?"* (ESV)

The admonition in Hebrew shows a marriage should remain intact regardless of acts of sexual immorality, even the ones that are not revealed. God is the faithful witness and will render to each of us, according to every single action. Hebrews 13:4 reads, *"Let marriage be held in honor among all, and let the marriage bed be undefiled, for God will judge the sexually immoral and adulterous."* (ESV)

27. The Lord said only the son of perdition was lost, which means Judas Iscariot went to hell and not paradise. How then could such a man be among the twelve disciples spoken of by the Lord, and yet he's known from the beginning by Him to be the very one who will be His betrayer? And still, the Lord makes the assertion found in Matthew 19:28, *"Jesus said to them, "Truly, I say to you, in the new world, when the Son of Man will sit on his glorious throne, you who have followed me will also sit on twelve thrones, judging the twelve tribes of Israel."* (ESV)

After having washed the disciples' feet the night He was betrayed, the Lord clearly stated who were His, as written in John 13:18: *"If you know these things, blessed are you if you do them. I am not speaking of all of you; I know whom I have chosen. But the Scripture will be fulfilled, 'He who ate my bread has lifted his heel against me.'"* (ESV)

The betrayer, Judas Iscariot, is clearly designated and excluded from the blessed panel. How could he become among those who will be seated on twelve thrones to judge Israel's tribes, knowing his place will be taken by Matthias, who at the time of those events hadn't yet been included with the eleven other apostles? As reads Acts 1:24–26, *"And they prayed and said, "You, Lord, who know the hearts of all, show which one of these two you have chosen to take the place in this ministry and apostleship from which Judas turned aside to go to his own place." And they cast lots for them, and the lot fell on Matthias, and he was numbered with the eleven apostles."* (ESV)

Take note: After the last supper, when the Lord explains to the disciples what will happen to Him, then prays for their ministry to succeed, as John reports in chapters 15–17, Judas Iscariot isn't among them and isn't receiving the blessings. Therefore, though that declaration sounds good and is even convincing, that's purely and simply another deceit since it's written in John 6:64: *"But there are some of you who do not believe." (For Jesus knew from the beginning who those were who did not believe, and who it was who would betray him.)"* (ESV)

Those who will indeed judge the tribes of Israel won't be only twelve, but these will be believers who would have by their faith overcome the world and endured tribulation. Those are the ones who will rule as powers, dominions, authorities with the Lord, and thus will lead the world's nations as it's prophesied by Jeremiah in 33:25–26: *"Thus says the LORD: If I have not established my covenant with day and night and the fixed order of heaven and earth, then I will reject the offspring of Jacob and David my servant and will not choose one of his offspring to rule over the offspring of Abraham, Isaac, and Jacob. For I will restore their fortunes and will have mercy on them."* (ESV)

The Christ is Lord over the whole of creation, not only Israel. Thus, his followers will rule the whole earth.

28. If we will inherit everything, that's not the purpose of our pursuit. We love God, meaning we act and think as He does because He's Holy, Faithful, and truthful. Thus, for all the love poured in our lives through numerous blessings, we enjoy serving Him and doing His commandments, which aren't burdensome. What's in the heart, His Holy Word is our treasure and what we nurture. When depicting our inheritance as material or making proclamations with numbers without foundation, this leads only to confusion. Surely, that's the aim of such author. As Matthew 19:29 reads, *"And everyone who has left houses or brothers or sisters or father or mother or children or lands, for my name's sake, will receive a hundredfold and will inherit eternal*

life." (ESV)

Many are missionaries who have left family and lands yet don't walk in the way of the Lord. That's not the condition that gives life eternal, but the keeping of God's commandments, by believing the Lord Jesus Christ is the Living Son of God. Moreover, it's written in Isaiah 61:6–7, "*you shall be called the priests of the Lord; they shall speak of you as the ministers of our God; you shall eat the wealth of the nations, and in their glory you shall boast. Instead of your shame there shall be a double portion; instead of dishonor they shall rejoice in their lot; therefore in their land they shall possess a double portion; they shall have everlasting joy.*" (ESV)

Furthermore, Mark 10:29 specified the reason for leaving is the Lord's Name and the Good News, while Luke 18:29, using the very same quote, states instead, "*for the sake of the Kingdom of God.*" Additionally, it's in the present time, meaning what will be gained in this world is the Church, with brothers and sisters, mothers and children. Take note that spouses aren't mentioned; rather this comes with persecutions. Truth is the reality and not a fantasy that will please many. Thus, true believers will join and evolve within the Church and endure trials like the Lord said: "*. . . If they persecuted me, they will also persecute you. . . .*" (NKJV) (John 15:20)

The wording of the Matthew story is purposely vague in order to entertain such misconception. The Kingdom of God isn't a stock market where people come to increase their wealth. That's the expression of a carnal mind and has nothing to do with God's children. Mark 10:29 reads, "*Jesus said, "Truly, I say to you, there is no one who has left house or brothers or sisters or mother or father or children or lands, for my sake and for the gospel, who will not receive a hundredfold now in this time, houses and brothers and sisters and mothers and children and lands, with persecutions, and in the age to come eternal life.*" (ESV)

29. If there is a place where meritocracy finds all its meaning, it's the Holy Kingdom of God. No favoritism will

ever happen, as God is infinitely just. Otherwise, Christ, for example, would have lived a completely different life on earth, free of hassle. The Parable found in Matthew 20:1–16 does not properly illustrate God's ruling. Another example reported by Luke in 21:1–4 provides the proper standpoint of the Lord. *"Jesus looked up and saw the rich putting their gifts into the offering box, and he saw a poor widow put in two small copper coins. And he said, 'Truly, I tell you, this poor widow has put in more than all of them. For they all contributed out of their abundance, but she out of her poverty put in all she had to live on.'"* (ESV)

It reminds of the sacrifices made by Cain and Abel. Cain offered the fruit of the ground, and Abel gave the firstborn of his flock and of their fat portions. We can see Abel didn't simply offer something to remove the weight of a requirement, but rather presented the best of what he had. The difference is how each one sees God: It's obvious for Abel He is to be revered as the Most High God, but not so for Cain, whose offering shows his contempt. The Lord Himself showed by His earthly existence how He valued His Father. His death on the cross is more than a testimony. His anguish in Gethsemane was another illustration of that utmost reverence toward His Father. His agony was of being separated for the first time ever from His Father. He declared in John 4:34, *"My food is to do the will of him who sent me and to accomplish his work."* (ESV)

Isaiah on the matter says in 11:2-3. *"The Spirit of the Lord shall rest upon Him, The Spirit of wisdom and understanding, The Spirit of counsel and might, The Spirit of knowledge and of the fear of the Lord. His delight is in the fear of the Lord, …"* (NKJV)

In a similar viewpoint, that's the reason why the apostle Paul advised believers to see others as above them: When you value someone, you consider such one in the best and suitable way possible. And this for Christians is to be accomplished with everyone, without any kind of distinction whatsoever. Again, the apostle Paul explained that principle in Romans 8:16–17: *"The Spirit himself bears witness with our spirit that we are children of*

God, and if children, then heirs—heirs of God and fellow heirs with Christ, provided we suffer with him in order that we may also be glorified with him." (ESV)

Likewise, in 2 Timothy 2:11–12, he writes, *"The saying is trustworthy, for: If we have died with him, we will also live with him; if we endure, we will also reign with him; if we deny him, he also will deny us;"* (ESV)

Also, in Colossians 3:23–25, it reads, *"Whatever you do, work heartily, as for the Lord and not for men, knowing that from the Lord you will receive the inheritance as your reward. You are serving the Lord Christ. For the wrongdoer will be paid back for the wrong he has done, and there is no partiality."* (ESV)

How then did the Matthew's author dare insert a parable showing partiality of the house's master, who paid the same amount of money to those who had labored all day long under the hot sun as those who did so for just one hour? And even pretend such is an image of the Holy Kingdom of God? Holy means all is done in truth and love. Why then are Christians persecuted in this earthly life, if not to be rewarded in the one that will follow? God could likewise spare His children or have them experience minimal unpleasantness. But was it the case for Christ Jesus, or the apostles and other prophets, or the various other faithful men of God? Hebrews 11:35–38 reads, *". . . Some were tortured, refusing to accept release, so that they might rise again to a better life. Others suffered mocking and flogging, and even chains and imprisonment. They were stoned, they were sawn in two, they were killed with the sword. They went about in skins of sheep and goats, destitute, afflicted, mistreated— of whom the world was not worthy— wandering about in deserts and mountains, and in dens and caves of the earth."* (ESV)

The Holy Kingdom of God is righteousness, peace, and joy in the Holy Spirit; that means love. It's written in Psalms 62:11–12 that the Holy God is Faithful and Just. *"Once God has spoken; twice have I heard this: that power belongs to God, and that to you, O Lord, belongs steadfast love. For you will render to a man according to his work."* (ESV)

The expression was used in Mark 10:31 but misused in Matthew 19:30, and 20:16 tells the reality of God's ruling. We may appear to be striving in this life, only to be at the bottom of the list in the one to come. God sees all, even what's in the darkness. That's why the apostle Paul said in 1 Corinthians 9:27, "*I discipline my body and keep it under control, lest after preaching to others I myself should be disqualified.*" (ESV)

The rules are the same for all, which the Holy God submitted Himself to—Christ is God. Therefore no one will be granted special treatment over others: Justice is fairness. All who will receive the inheritance would have fought per the same rules. Thus, the apostle Paul said in 2 Timothy 4:7–8, "*I have fought the good fight, I have finished the race, I have kept the faith. Henceforth there is laid up for me the crown of righteousness, which the Lord, the righteous judge, will award to me on that day, and not only to me but also to all who have loved his appearing.*" (ESV)

30. Why should the mother of the sons of Zebedee make the request on behalf of the two brothers, who are no longer children, as it's written in Matthew 20:20–21? The original version states in Mark 10:35–37, "*And James and John, the sons of Zebedee, came up to him and said to him, 'Teacher, we want you to do for us whatever we ask of you.' And he said to them, 'What do you want me to do for you?' And they said to him, 'Grant us to sit, one at your right hand and one at your left, in your glory.'*" (ESV)

What's the purpose of placing a woman in front of these two for this request to the Lord? What connotation is being conveyed? Why twist the original text by these incongruent details, bringing only misperception? Luke 11:27-28 shows the Lord's perspective on this school of thought that began in Eden with Eve. "*As he said these things, a woman in the crowd raised her voice and said to him, "Blessed is the womb that bore you, and the breasts at which you nursed!" But he said, "Blessed rather are those who hear the word of God and keep it!"*" (ESV)

31. The Lord, hungry on the way to Jerusalem, cursed a fig tree that had only leaves, according to Mark 11:14: *"And he said to it, 'May no one ever eat fruit from you again.' And his disciples heard it."* (ESV)

Verses 11:20–24 recount the following morning: *"As they passed by in the morning, they saw the fig tree withered away to its roots. And Peter remembered and said to him, 'Rabbi, look! The fig tree that you cursed has withered.' And Jesus answered them, 'Have faith in God. Truly, I say to you, whoever says to this mountain, 'Be taken up and thrown into the sea,' and does not doubt in his heart, but believes that what he says will come to pass, it will be done for him. Therefore I tell you, whatever you ask in prayer, believe that you have received it, and it will be yours.'"* (ESV)

Matthew's story instead gives a totally different version that raises suspicion and even astonishes, as if Christ Jesus was a magician, as written in verses 21:19–20: *"And seeing a fig tree by the wayside, he went to it and found nothing on it but only leaves. And he said to it, 'May no fruit ever come from you again!' And the fig tree withered at once. When the disciples saw it, they marveled, saying, 'How did the fig tree wither at once?'"* (ESV)

The version of Mark is upheld by a previous event with Jonah after his sojourn in the fish's belly, then the prophecy in Nineveh. It's written in Jonah 4:10, "And the LORD said, *"You pity the plant, for which you did not labor, nor did you make it grow, which came into being in a night and perished in a night."* (ESV)

Like it was in the desert with the rod of Aaron, as reads Numbers 17:7–8, *"And Moses deposited the staffs before the LORD in the tent of the testimony. On the next day Moses went into the tent of the testimony, and behold, the staff of Aaron for the house of Levi had sprouted and put forth buds and produced blossoms, and it bore ripe almonds."* (ESV)

Note: It's important to understand that the Lord could do what is said in Matthew, just as He could have opened the Red Sea in a split second with Moses, and performed many other miracles in an impressive way: He is Almighty. As He said to the prophet Jeremiah in 32:27. *"Behold, I am the Lord, the God of all flesh. Is anything too hard for me?"* (ESV) Just as He told Abraham, before Sarah then aged eighty-nine years, gave birth to her first son Isaac in Genesis 18:13-14. *"The Lord said to Abraham, 'Why did Sarah laugh and say, 'Shall I indeed bear a child, now that I am old?' Is anything too hard for the Lord? At the appointed time I will return to you, about this time next year, and Sarah shall have a son.'"* (ESV)

If He didn't go beyond a certain point, it was because He wanted to lead our faith by raising it gradually. He told Nicodemus in John 3:12. *"If I have told you earthly things and you do not believe, how can you believe if I tell you heavenly things?"* (ESV) Just as he said to His apostles on the night of His betrayal, *"I still have many things to say to you, but you cannot bear them now."* (ESV) (John 16:12). Thus, there are many things we cannot understand and so, to allow a weak faith to grow gradually, He guides our consciousness through things we can bear and are accustomed to.

The author of Matthew willingly accentuates certain details to make the story sound like a fantasy, which is the best way to deny the Lord: pretending to believe but providing such a hard-to-believe untruth. And pushing the envelope even further, he states the Lord told disciples they could do the same with faith. But in whom should they have faith to do such a thing? What kind of teaching is being presented to readers? It reads in 1 Timothy 4:1–2, *"Now the Spirit expressly says that in later times some will depart from the faith by devoting themselves to deceitful spirits and teachings of demons, through the insincerity of liars whose consciences are seared,"* (ESV)

The following story in verses 21:23–27 is placed in such a manner that it accentuates the suspicion about the origin of the Lord's power. After the fig tree that withered instantly, the reply found in verse 21:27 unconsciously raises doubts: *"So they answered Jesus, 'We do not know.' And he said to them, 'Neither will I tell you by what authority I do these things.'"* (ESV)

Just like a cunning fictional plot in a crime novel, this story is conceived to dismantle a believer's assurance. It's interesting to notice the original version has a different parable that follows, which clearly depicts Jesus' betrayal by the spiritual leaders, in Mark 12:1–12. Likewise, Luke in verses 20:9–19 follows Mark's parable. This proves that Matthew unfolds has a concealed intention: a design conceived only to mislead people.

32. The parable found in Luke 14:16–22 is transformed in an act of vengeance by the author of Matthew in 22:1–14. If Luke explained what is the Lord's invitation to abide in His love, which all despisers will dearly regret when facing the reality of eternity, it's distorted in Matthew where added details make these opposants worthy of death and their city to be burned, though all of them have not mistreated and killed the servants of the king mentioned. If an eternity in the lake of fire and brimstone is their lot, none will be forced to enter God's Kingdom: life is a choice, not an obligation. Moreover, nothing defiled will ever enter the Holy city of Zion in heaven, as the Matthew parable alleges in verses 22:11–13. If some will indeed be removed from the Kingdom as Luke illustrated in 13:24–28, such are the ones pretending to be Christians but who haven't kept the commandments, rather walked according to the tradition of this world. Thus, these are of the devil and seen as "be leavers" who never experience tribulations, as being part of the world, having a carnal mind, as explained in 2 Timothy 3:5: *"having the appearance of godliness, but denying its power. Avoid such people."* (ESV)

33. It's intriguing to see how many times context is bent in Matthew's verses, which report what the mindset of a leader is, per the Lord's standards in 23:11. *"The greatest among you shall be your servant."* (ESV)

That parable is expounded in Luke's account that states in

verses 22:26–27, "*But not so with you. Rather, let the greatest among you become as the youngest, and the leader as one who serves. For who is the greater, one who reclines at table or one who serves? Is it not the one who reclines at table? But I am among you as the one who serves.*" (ESV)

Likewise, in Mark's account, the Lord explained after the sons of Zebedee requested to be seated at His right-hand and left-hand side, anyone who desires to be the greatest of all must be the minister of all, as written in Mark 10:43–44. "*But it shall not be so among you. But whoever would be great among you must be your servant, and whoever would be first among you must be slave of all.*" (ESV)

Though Mark's version is closer to Matthew's, it still shows it's a figure of speech, whereas in Matthew, it's an affirmation that changes the context. It gives the impression one must be slave or servant to be the leader, which in reality is the behavior one must have toward others, as the apostle explained in 1 Peter 5:1–3. "*So I exhort the elders among you, as a fellow elder and a witness of the sufferings of Christ, as well as a partaker in the glory that is going to be revealed: shepherd the flock of God that is among you, exercising oversight, not under compulsion, but willingly, as God would have you; not for shameful gain, but eagerly; not domineering over those in your charge, but being examples to the flock.*" (ESV)

The example of the congregation, just as the Lord has been for His disciples in all things, even to His death.

34. Whenever confusion appears, one must acknowledge the devil's footprint. One of Luke's quotes is reiterated in Matthew 23:35 as such: "*so that on you may come all the righteous blood shed on earth, from the blood of righteous Abel to the blood of Zechariah the son of Barachiah, whom you murdered between the sanctuary and the altar.*" (ESV)

There are numerous people with that first name in the Bible; however, other than the prophet Zechariah whose surname matches almost perfectly, as "*the son of Berechiah*" (Zechariah 1:1), only two others draw attention. One is the son of the high priest Jehoiada, who was killed in the temple of the Lord, as written in 2 Chronicles 24:21–22. *"But they conspired against him, and by command of the king they stoned him with stones in the court of the house of the Lord. Thus Joash the king did not remember the kindness that Jehoiada, Zechariah's father, had shown him, but killed his son. And when he was dying, he said, "May the Lord see and avenge!"* (ESV)

The other one is found in the book of Isaiah the prophet in 8:2. It's the sound of his name that makes one notice. But not much is said about him other than having been of the prophet Isaiah's two faithful witnesses. *"And I will get reliable witnesses, Uriah the priest and Zechariah the son of Jeberechiah, to attest for me."* (ESV)

The quote that is found in Luke 11:51 doesn't state the victim's surname: *"from the blood of Abel to the blood of Zechariah, who perished between the altar and the sanctuary. Yes, I tell you, it will be required of this generation."* (ESV)

Knowing that the accounts of Luke and Mark are the sources of the author of Matthew, why add this ambiguity, if not to deceive? There is no mention in the whole Bible of a prophet Zechariah, son of Barachiah being murdered in the Lord's temple.

35. It's written in Matthew 24:12, *"And because lawlessness will be increased, the love of many will grow cold."* (ESV)

No other author of the Good News made that affirmation. What's its objective? Is it a false prophecy as the one of the cities of Judah, who won't be all evangelized, that the Son of God had returned? Time has showed and history ratifies it's a pure lie, like so many claims of this falsity. Is it an incitement to become what's said?

36. The parable of the ten virgins sounds accurate and even clever. However, there's an issue of justice that must be addressed. We are behind enemy lines as Christian believers on earth. Like any other army, no soldier will ever be

abandoned on the battlefield. That's the reason why, with compassion toward others, we invite them to acknowledge the Lord's teachings, which will save the souls of those who have believed. Consequently, it would make sense that such a heart's disposition be manifested by the five wise ones, which should've advised the foolish beforehand to gather more oil just in case they had to wait longer than expected. Because the foolish ask afterward, it demonstrates these steps were apparently missing in the events' unfoldment. Once again, a depiction of the world's functioning is presented as being the one of the Holy Kingdom of God. The fact this has occurred often proves it's not an oversight but a willful attempt to mislead and present what's evil as being good and portraying Holiness as wickedness. Such was what the serpent accomplished in Eden, and yet the same trick is still used with a certain success, sadly. That parable is found only in Matthew's account, in verses 25:1–23. Like other added information, it's inserted in a section of the original report.

37. Matthew 25:31–46 relates the parable of sheep and goats. What's the purpose of setting all these on the stage, only to have the righteous go on to life eternal and the remaining to damnation? What lesson must be drawn from that explanation?

38. Manifold deceits are affirmed throughout the story of Matthew, opposing various other records, like the leak of the betrayer's name during the supper, which the apostle John, an eyewitness, clearly described and stated no one understood what the Lord said to Judas in John 13:24–28. *"Simon Peter therefore motioned to him to ask who it was of whom He spoke. Then, leaning back on Jesus' breast, he said to Him, 'Lord, who is it?' Jesus answered, 'It is he to whom I shall give a piece of bread when I have dipped it.' And having dipped the bread, He gave it to Judas Iscariot, the son of Simon. Now after the piece of bread, Satan entered him. Then Jesus said*

to him, 'What you do, do quickly.'" But no one at the table knew for what reason He said this to him." (NKJV)

However, Matthew's story declares the Lord specifically designated Judas Iscariot as such through His actions and precisely while they were eating, as reads verses 26:21–23: "And as they were eating, he said, 'Truly, I say to you, one of you will betray me.' And they were very sorrowful and began to say to him one after another, 'Is it I, Lord' He answered, 'He who has dipped his hand in the dish with me will betray me.'" (ESV)

Moreover, in 26:25, it reads, "Judas, who would betray him, answered, 'Is it I, Rabbi?' He said to him, 'You have said so.'" (ESV)

That version contradicts what's written in Proverbs 25:9–10 by Solomon, whose wisdom was given by God. Would the Lord contradict Himself and teach us lies? "Argue your case with your neighbor himself, and do not reveal another's secret, lest he who hears you bring shame upon you, and your ill repute have no end." (ESV)

39. The reckon of Judas's acts regarding the money and field of his crime contradict others, like Peter's version found in the book of Acts in 1:16–19: "'Brothers, the Scripture had to be fulfilled, which the Holy Spirit spoke beforehand by the mouth of David concerning Judas, who became a guide to those who arrested Jesus. For he was numbered among us and was allotted his share in this ministry.' (Now this man acquired a field with the reward of his wickedness, and falling headlong he burst open in the middle and all his bowels gushed out. And it became known to all the inhabitants of Jerusalem, so that the field was called in their own language Akeldama, that is, Field of Blood.)" (ESV)

If Judas bought the field, then fell headlong, how come he brought back the full amount to the Pharisees, who used it to buy a field as a burial place? Did he hang himself before or after his bowels gushed out when he burst open in the middle? For Matthew 27:3–5 reads, "Then when Judas, his betrayer, saw that Jesus was condemned, he changed his mind and brought back the thirty pieces of silver to the chief priests and the elders, saying, 'I have sinned by *betraying innocent blood.' They said, 'What is that to us? See to it yourself.' And throwing down the pieces of silver into the temple, he departed, and he went and hanged himself."* (ESV)

As per Peter's version, Judas didn't repent; rather he went on and used that money to buy a field.

Even the prophecy reference that used Jeremiah, not Zechariah 11:13, is wrong; in the whole Bible, nowhere is this kind of awkwardness found. Matthew 27:6–10 reads, *"But the chief priests, taking the pieces of silver, said, 'It is not lawful to put them into the treasury, since it is blood money.' So they took counsel and bought with them the potter's field as a burial place for strangers. Therefore that field has been called the Field of Blood to this day. Then was fulfilled what had been spoken by the prophet Jeremiah, saying, 'And they took the thirty pieces of silver, the price of him on whom a price had been set by some of the sons of Israel, and they gave them for the potter's field, as the Lord directed me.'"* (ESV)

If the chief priests bought a field with Judas's money, what did he use to buy his own, which was called a "field of blood"? The reference wrongly mentioned is found in Zechariah 11:13: *"Then the LORD said to me, 'Throw it to the potter'—the lordly price at which I was priced by them. So I took the thirty pieces of silver and threw them into the house of the LORD, to the potter."* (ESV)

40. What does the saying imply in Matthew 27:19? *"Besides, while he was sitting on the judgment seat, his wife sent word to him, 'Have nothing to do with that righteous man, for I have suffered much because of him today in a dream.'"* (ESV)

Her admonition sounds more like a prophetic message to guide the man in his decision. If she has suffered because of the Lord in a dream, which side is she on? God or the devil?

Once again, we see this tendency to put women first in order to grant them a certain notoriety. We must remember that the devil's plan is to reverse God's order, as with Eve before Adam, for example. As a result, the "legends faction" believes in matriarchy and therefore seeks to impose women by any means necessary. However, Isaiah prophesied as follows on this subject in 3:12. *"As for My people, children are their oppressors, And women rule over them. O My people! Those who lead you cause you to err, And destroy the way of your paths.'"* (ESV)

Per Luke 13:1–2, Pilate is a pagan idolator who abuses his power. *"There were some present at that very time who told him about the Galileans whose blood Pilate had mingled with their sacrifices. And he answered them, 'Do you think that these Galileans were worse sinners than all the other Galileans, because they suffered in this way?'"* (ESV)

41. Matthew's account is the only one stating Pilate washed his hands and declared himself to be innocent of Jesus' blood. Then the crowd replied His blood should be upon them and their children, as written in verses 27:24–25: *"So when Pilate saw that he was gaining nothing, but rather that a riot was beginning, he took water and washed his hands before the crowd, saying, 'I am innocent of this man's blood; see to it yourselves.' And all the people answered, 'His blood be on us and on our children!'"* (ESV)

Per John 19:11 that reads, *"Jesus answered him, 'You would have no authority over me at all unless it had been given you from above. Therefore he who delivered me over to you has the greater sin.'"* (ESV)

Pilate therefore knew he wasn't at all innocent in that matter, especially because he knew it was by envy that the priests had delivered the Lord. Therefore, Pilate's judgment was wrong and based only on his advantages, as he found it more appealing to be in Caesar's good graces than God's.

42. The saints' resurrection set alongside Jesus' can't fit with the Lord's teachings, conveyed by His apostles, for the Matthew story states in verses 27:51–53, *"Then, behold, the veil of the temple was torn in two from top to bottom; and the earth quaked, and the rocks were split, and the graves were opened; and many bodies of the saints who had fallen asleep were raised; and coming out of the graves after His resurrection, they went into the holy city and appeared to many."* (NKJV)

What events unfolded here? At the moment the Lord died, the earth quaked and graves were thus opened, with saints' bodies brought back to life. But they had to wait three days to exit these graves, only after Jesus' resurrection? Were they fasting in their graves while patiently waiting for the right time to settle? There is no logic in these rantings. And what happened after they've appeared to those numerous ones, who forgot to testify about that rare event? Did they die again or ascend to heaven with the Lord? It's evident this portion of that story was written to create disbelief in the mind of all faithful readers.

The letter sent to Hebrews explains all those who died even before the Christ's advent on earth, thereby all righteous who have walked with God from Abel until now, will not reach the perfection before us, as reads 11:39–40: *"And all these, though commended through their faith, did not receive what was promised, since God had provided something better for us, that apart from us they should not be made perfect."* (ESV)

The apostle Paul explains the chronology of events when all of Jesus' martyrs will rise from death in his first letter sent to the Thessalonians in 4:15–17: *"For this we say to you by the word of the Lord, that we who are alive and remain until the coming of the Lord will by no means precede those who are asleep. For the Lord Himself will descend from heaven with a shout, with the voice of an archangel, and with the trumpet of God. And the dead in Christ will rise first. Then we who are alive and remain shall be caught up together with them in the clouds to meet the Lord in the air. And thus we shall always be with the Lord."* (NKJV)

And again, in a second letter to Timothy, he criticizes those who teach other doctrines, as written in 2:16–18. *"But shun profane and idle babblings, for they will increase to more ungodliness. And their message will spread like cancer. Hymenaeus and Philetus are of this sort, who have strayed concerning the truth, saying that the resurrection is already past; and they overthrow the faith of some."* (NKJV)

How is Matthew's author different from those spoken

about by the apostle Paul?

43. Only Matthew version stipulates the mother of Zebedee's sons was among the women who served the Lord. After her intrusion in the story when she brought her sons before the Lord, requesting to have them seated at His right-hand and left-hand side, here she is brought back by the author in verse 27:55-56, *"There were also many women there, looking on from a distance, who had followed Jesus from Galilee, ministering to him, among whom were Mary Magdalene and Mary the mother of James and Joseph and the mother of the sons of Zebedee."* (ESV) Luke resumed that section of Mark's account with a different terminology. Matthew's author therefore used Mark's material to craft his and changed the casting. Mark 15:40 reads, *"There were also women looking on from a distance, among whom were Mary Magdalene, and Mary the mother of James the younger and of Joses, and Salome."* (ESV)

44. Both of Matthew's author's sources describe Joseph of Arimathea as a respected member of the Council for Mark's version in verse 15:43 and, per Luke's version, a member of the council, a good and righteous man. It is obvious by these two accounts he is of the council and an upright one. However, Matthew's author made him a rich man—knowing that the meaning of a rich person back then was per the explanation found in verses 5:1–6 of James's exhortation, which explains that these rich people exploited poor ones without mercy and often made them work without salary. It is an image totally different from the one provided by Mark and Luke. This also implies that these kinds of people were the Lord's kin, with all hypotheses such rhetoric brings to one's mind. Matthew 27:57–60 says, *"When it was evening, there came a rich man from Arimathea, named Joseph, who also was a disciple of Jesus. He went to Pilate and asked for the body of Jesus. Then Pilate ordered it to be given to him. And Joseph took the body and wrapped it in a clean*

linen shroud and laid it in his own new tomb, which he had cut in the rock. And he rolled a great stone to the entrance of the tomb and went away." (ESV)

Besides, the apostle John, who was an eyewitness, specified in his account in verses 19:38–42, *"After these things Joseph of Arimathea, who was a disciple of Jesus, but secretly for fear of the Jews, asked Pilate that he might take away the body of Jesus, and Pilate gave him permission. So he came and took away his body. Nicodemus also, who earlier had come to Jesus by night, came bringing a mixture of myrrh and aloes, about seventy-five pounds in weight. So they took the body of Jesus and bound it in linen cloths with the spices, as is the burial custom of the Jews. Now in the place where he was crucified there was a garden, and in the garden a new tomb in which no one had yet been laid. So because of the Jewish day of Preparation, since the tomb was close at hand, they laid Jesus there."* (ESV)

Not only does he confirm Joseph was of the council, he even provides a corroborating clue, saying he was a disciple of the Lord in secret, by fear of the Jews. On top of that, Mark also validates these facts when stating he dared go to Pilate and asked for the body, in 15:43: *"Joseph of Arimathea, a respected member of the Council, who was also himself looking for the kingdom of God, took courage and went to Pilate and asked for the body of Jesus."* (ESV)

Thus, Joseph was among them, but not participating to their evil machinations, as Luke specified in verses 23:50–51, *"Now there was a man named Joseph, from the Jewish town of Arimathea. He was a member of the council, a good and righteous man, who had not consented to their decision and action; and he was looking for the kingdom of God."* (ESV)

Also, contrary to Matthew's version, the tomb was used because of its proximity, and wasn't one that the rich man made cut in the rock—for when would he have made it cut? Did he know Christ would be crucified there, or did these workers provided an express labor and cut the tomb in the rock in a few minutes? Joseph is of Arimathea, but his tomb is in Jerusalem. Back then, people were buried wherever they died since body preservation wasn't available, other than Egyptian mummification taking about forty days in their land. Matthew's version in no way can stand an accuracy test. The fact the tomb was nearby supports Mary's request to the Lord after His resurrection, thinking it was the gardener speaking to her, as reads John 20:15" *"Jesus said to her, 'Woman, why are you weeping? Whom are you seeking?' Supposing him to be the gardener, she said to him, 'Sir, if you have carried him away, tell me where you have laid him, and I will take him away.'"* (ESV)

This implies the Lord's body had been laid in that sepulcher, probably without the consent of the owner. As no one is supposed to work on the Sabbath, it would have remained there unnoticed, then arrangements would have been made afterward to have it laid in a more suitable and secured place. Thus, the panic when the body was missing on the first day of the week when they came to anoint it. That owner could have asked the gardener to dispose of that unknown cadaver, which was laid in his propriety without his approval.

45. Matthew's story is the only one mentioning guards keeping the Lord's sepulcher. Surely, these details are needed to provide a groundwork for the epilogue of that scheme: deny the Lord's resurrection, which also tacitly refutes His whole story, thus existence. Take note that when they go to Pilate, the author literally puts words in the reader's mind. Indeed, some uphold such a version of facts to this day. Verses 27:62–66 read, *"The next day, that is, after the day of Preparation, the chief priests and the Pharisees gathered before Pilate and said, "Sir, we remember how that impostor said, while he was still alive, 'After three days I will rise.' Therefore order the tomb to be made secure until the third day, lest his disciples go and steal him away and tell the people, 'He has risen from the dead,' and the last fraud will be worse than the first." Pilate said to them, "You have a guard of soldiers. Go, make it as secure as you can." So they went and made the tomb secure by sealing the stone and*

setting a guard." (ESV)

46. How many earthquakes happened in those days? The day of Lord's death, then again two days after. And yet it seems they only affect the places where they happen, as no effect is reported elsewhere. Even the description of the angel is singular in the whole Bible. If white clothes are often depicted, appearance like lightning is a Matthew's story exclusivity. Angels don't appear to the mischievous, but to the righteous. Just like demons are seen by evil ones and not upright ones: they just don't communicate. Daniel explained what happened to those who were with him when the angel of the Lord appeared, in verses 10:5–7. *"I lifted up my eyes and looked, and behold, a man clothed in linen, with a belt of fine gold from Uphaz around his waist. His body was like beryl, his face like the appearance of lightning, his eyes like flaming torches, his arms and legs like the gleam of burnished bronze, and the sound of his words like the sound of a multitude. And I, Daniel, alone saw the vision, for the men who were with me did not see the vision, but a great trembling fell upon them, and they fled to hide themselves."* (ESV)

If the face is like lightning, the body is different. This description translates the face of the Lord that shines with His Glory.

The guards in Matthew became like dead men, yet saw and heard everything, for they went to the priests and reported the whole matter? They then fell down unconscious with their eyes wide open?

Jesus' meeting with women coming to anoint His body is inaccurate. It is contrary to John's teachings as someone who was an eyewitness to the events. Its unfolding hasn't the Biblical proof that John's report has with Haggai's prophecy in 2:12–13, the Lord couldn't be touched before ascending to the Father; a Holy sacrifice being soiled by a dead body, what we all are as it's written. *"'If one carries holy meat in the fold of his garment, and with the edge he touches bread or stew, wine or oil, or any food, will it become holy?' Then the priests answered and said, 'No.' And Haggai said, 'If one who is unclean because of a dead body touches any of these, will it be unclean' So the priests answered and said, 'It shall be unclean.'"* (NKJV)

Our dead status is shown with John 14:19, for example. *"Yet a little while and the world will see me no more, but you will see me. Because I live, you also will live."* (ESV)

The Lord said, *"I live,"* but for the disciples, it's not yet a reality, therefore He says, *"You also will live."* How? When the Holy Spirit comes to our heart. The apostle Paul explains this reality in his Ephesians letter in verses 2:1–5. *"And you He made alive, who were dead in trespasses and sins, in which you once walked according to the course of this world, according to the prince of the power of the air, the spirit who now works in the sons of disobedience, among whom also we all once conducted ourselves in the lusts of our flesh, fulfilling the desires of the flesh and of the mind, and were by nature children of wrath, just as the others. But God, who is rich in mercy, because of His great love with which He loved us, even when we were dead in trespasses, made us alive together with Christ (by grace you have been saved),"* (NKJV)

Adam and Eve died in Eden when they sinned. Such is the image we've inherited from Adam, different from that of God, as written in Genesis 5:3. *"And Adam lived one hundred and thirty years, and begot a son in his own likeness, after his image, and named him Seth."* (NKJV)

Adam's spirit was dead because of his sin, contrary to the Spirit of God, Who has often reiterated in His dialogue with the various prophets that He lives. Like He said to Ezekiel in 33:11, *"Say to them: 'As I live,' says the Lord GOD, 'I have no pleasure in the death of the wicked, but that the wicked turn from his way and live. Turn, turn from your evil ways! For why should you die, O house of Israel?'"* (NKJV)

Take note the death spoken of here is the second one, after Judgment Day, before the Throne of the Lord Jesus. It's therefore death of the soul, which is the reward of all those who refuse redemption through love and prefer to live in hatred, far from God and His Word.

47. Even the very last sentence of that story is wrong, as reads verse 28:20. "". . . *And behold, I am with you always, to the end of the age.*"" (ESV)

When the Lord comes back, He will appear only to faithful ones for all to be reunited in the clouds for an everlasting ministry in heaven. If the Lord is with us through the Holy Spirit, we will never be separated from Him. Consequently, in this earthly existence, the Lord abides in us by His Holy Spirit. Then in the age to come, we will serve Him forever, leading all nations in God's way as powers, authorities, dominions. It's written in Luke 1:73–75: "*the oath that he swore to our father Abraham, to grant us that we, being delivered from the hand of our enemies, might serve him without fear, in holiness and righteousness before him all our days.*" (ESV)

Revelation 7:14–17 reads, ". . . *These are the ones coming out of the great tribulation. They have washed their robes and made them white in the blood of the Lamb. Therefore they are before the throne of God, and serve him day and night in his temple; and he who sits on the throne will shelter them with his presence. They shall hunger no more, neither thirst anymore; the sun shall not strike them, nor any scorching heat. For the Lamb in the midst of the throne will be their shepherd, and he will guide them to springs of living water, and God will wipe away every tear from their eyes.*"" (ESV)

5 AMBIVALENCE

Though it seems hard to believe, it's evident that until now, those working at concealing the truth have succeeded in making the first account of the New Testament look like the apostle Matthew's genuine report. Some who challenge its numerous errors, never question its authenticity, rather dive often in senseless hypothesizes, while most on the other hand, find in theological sermons, various reasons to justify these discrepancies so blatant and out of all common sense, only deception can explain the intention of such aberrations. Thus, the consensus around its legitimacy and the tremendous amount of writings about its misunderstood theology, only prove the work of the "legends faction", drowning the fish in water.

It's impossible with the number of Bible readers having studied God's Word to have missed these errors. Rather than being inexistent, it's safe to think they have been muffled and their messages discarded. And today, with the internet, it's even easier to index one's message in such way no one ever sees it on the web. Not only can the author be isolated with devices that have been hijacked and are remotely controlled, but the access to internet websites is similarly restricted in such a way that pretty much all attempts are done in vain. In time past, having a publishing house was hard enough even for popular writers, how much more with the niche market that represents the Bible, with moreover, such controversial theme? And even if a book could be printed, the distribution channel would be another major roadblock because most of these entities are active members of veiled clubs. Therefore, it's evident these will only prevent the propagation of such information, as all being of the same obedience and part of this lasting scandalous shame for all humanity.

Per some definitions found on the internet, apocryphal implies an unknown or dubious source or origin. Using this definition as a starting point, the Matthew story is definitely of that category, since it's clear an eyewitness of the Lord's ministry would not plagiarize as did the author of that story. In that regard, Luke's account differs by the introduction stating he did research to provide a chronological unfolding of what happened. Thereby, it's evident that the facts provided have a different source and are not from him, which isn't said in the story named Matthew.

Moreover, Luke's account is a writing sent to a person desiring to know more about the Lord, thus Luke is doing what he saw the apostle Paul achieve in his ministry: testify about the Lord and impart God's wisdom. Mark's account is definitely the main source of both reports, and its content and teachings aren't foreign to the Lord's. However, as first recipient of the eyewitness—the apostle Peter, the shortage of details puzzles. All hypotheses will only be guesses we will avoid here. However, Luke, knowing Mark closely and being backed by Paul, shows his report is trustworthy and recognized by Luke as his genuine knowledge by using it. In John's account, it's clearly stated he wrote what is reported, thus its narrative is from a different person relating the apostle's memoires. The Matthew story is the only one standing without explanation nor known author, and rather have the claim from Papias of Hierapolis, who apparently wrote that Matthew "put together the oracles in the Hebrew language, and each one interpreted them as best he could," in a manuscript that has been lost and is only known as "the fragments of Papias." [7;8]

It seems that other early church fathers such as Pantaenus, Origen, and Irenaeus could also have confirmed Matthew as the author of the Gospel.

However, since all of this is contradicted by the common sense of an eyewitness who plagiarizes, it is deemed highly unlikely. Besides, the claimant can be of the "legends faction" or simply a corrupted member of the clergy, as several were.

Another criterion of the apocrypha is its tendency for falsification or deception. Many occurrences in Matthew clearly demonstrate such propensity. From the genealogy of which most names can't be found elsewhere in the Bible—invented personages, unless the shepherds of Luke in their way to Bethlehem became mages, which would definitely be demonstrated only in a fantasy, not in an account found in the Bible, relating historical facts. Invented parables that are presented as depicting God's ruling, but are in total opposition with all His teachings, demonstrate thereby that not only is it skillfully designed, it shows the author is an erudite applying a prearranged methodology planned to target the foundation of the Lord's doctrine. It's not like many comments try to portray the author as someone who knew very little about the Jewish culture and customs. When carefully examined, it's evident a willful intent to deceive in a very cunning way was implemented. With the amount of PhDs and other scholars who study the Bible, plus the controversies of the reformation and all its discourses, no one questioned that book nor its place as the first account to start the New Testament. The author is only one link of a chain laboring at destroying the truth. And the various campaigns of defamation, or various outlaw prohibitions to even pronounce the name of the Lord Jesus Christ, or make a comment about Him in any academic entity, with all these irrelevant comments about that falsity, are just other links of that chain.

The various added parables and persons of that story makes it likewise fall under the legendary criteria. These are pure inventions, yet always in perfect contradiction with the Lord's teachings. The mages are sorcerers, and they are led by a star, clearly things that the Lord ostensibly reproved. Nothing is said by error. It is rather a deliberate intention to convey an opposed doctrine, thus an attempt to switch iniquity with virtues that the Lord imparts to us in His Holy Word. The alleged sojourn of the Lord in Egypt was once again forcefully reproved by the Lord in many instances. And yet God Himself does it: In other words, that author tries to teach the reader that the Bible is about doing what the Lord says, but not what He does. Has this ever been God's position? Why then did the Christ suffer afflictions of all sorts on earth and finally die on the cross? In His infinite justice, God Himself came to earth to show the Way everlasting. That is who the Messiah is who died on the cross for us. Just as a teacher who has been through a lesson will solve the problem in front of the students as a demonstration of his point, in the same way Jesus paved the way to the Father in heaven.

The use of double instances for donkey or blind beggar is nothing else but a deformation of the reality, which only contributes to discredit the whole story and make the reader doubt of the genuineness of the Bible.

Is that story mythical, with its purely fanciful explanations of facts and creation of events sprung from the imagination? It definitely is fictitious at various points. And yet each time, the deceit represents something that has been cast as sinful, or it's a teaching that goes against one of the Lord. The Christ couldn't be touched before ascending to the Father, which John clearly states. But Matthew has women hold His feet, thereby meaning that an unholy body was presented in heaven for atonement. In other words, you are still in your sins. He died in vain, or, better yet, that whole story is only pure invention. Regardless of ways a reader will look at it, there will be a drawback making it worthless, and that's the intent of Matthew's author. If some deceits are subtle, others are obvious, while in some cases, they are just too much. Yet the question remains: How could all these be accepted by these innumerable Bible versions—especially in English and throughout centuries—by several Church leaders? Surely, at some point, the Church was thoroughly corrupted, which means these elders had long forsaken the Holy Spirit. Thus, earthly considerations only mattered.

Aside from the Inquisitions, which revealed the obvious misdirection of the clergy, another glaring example of this departure from common sense and reason is the neglect of the wealth of knowledge. If we consider, for example, what is advised in the hygiene rules of Leviticus, which clearly indicate how to prevent the spread of infectious diseases and thus pandemics. Despite this valuable information available to the Church, history bears witness to the catastrophe that was the Black Death, which decimated half the population of Europe, also affecting North Africa and Western Asia. Incompetence, negligence or ignorance? It has been established that it was not until about 1846 that the washing of hands in a medical context was introduced in Europe. However, around 1271 BC, Moses already advised the following in verse 15:13 of Leviticus. ". . . *he shall count for himself seven days for his cleansing, wash his clothes, and bathe his body in running water; then he shall be clean.*" (NKJV)

As a result, we are left with the following daunting but

relevant question: Why neglect such an important source of information?

When views differ, objectives are dissimilar, and, thus, the motivation and means diverge. The various schisms in the Church only show human intellect has replaced the Holy Spirit, as the apostle Paul discloses it in 1 Corinthians 3:1-4. *"And I, brethren, could not speak to you as to spiritual people but as to carnal, as to babes in Christ. I fed you with milk and not with solid food; for until now you were not able to receive it, and even now you are still not able; for you are still carnal. For where there are envy, strife, and divisions among you, are you not carnal and behaving like mere men? For when one says, "I am of Paul," and another, "I am of Apollos," are you not carnal?"* (NKJV)

Hence, the perception changes as goals evolve in a different direction. Consequently, the discourse follows. It's evident the Church has been taken hostage by foes, as many apostles have prophesied. The battle of influence around the wording of the writings, not fulfilling the criteria of deemed inspired scriptures in essence say only one thing: This does not belong to the Wisdom of God, for it is dubious and uncertain. Even in the definition, some assert these documents should not be used to impart doctrines in the church service or be read in public, but only in private for personal knowledge. Does it save a soul? Why not then also advise reading fantasies? The debate is willingly displaced to allow vain babbling and futile conjecture to simply waste people's time and, in conclusion, make us end up with an apocrypha account named Matthew as the first book in the New Testament. If many books named apocrypha or deuterocanonical by Catholics, and all other alternative names are not found easily in one category, it's obviously because some of them are questionable, while some of those selecting for the categories of these books aren't of good faith—in all the various implications of that expression. The Church of all times has been corrupted—the Lord's crucifixion is the result of that evidence, and some scribes already were criticized, as declared Jeremiah in verse 8:8. *"How can you say, 'We are wise, and the law of the LORD is with us'? But behold, the lying pen of the scribes has made it into a lie."* (ESV)

Our lack of knowledge is explained plainly in 1 Corinthians 13:9, which reads, *"For we know in part and we prophesy in part,"* (ESV) Since we know only in part and our lives' countless defects prove it, how could some believe self-will and human wisdom is above that of the Holy Spirit of the Living God, who made the whole creation? From the infinitely small to the infinitely big, of which we haven't begun to understand the Genesis. It's evident that the enemies of the Lord are those who have defined themselves as Christian bodies of all sorts, and many of the clergy through epochs held a like opinion: They had nothing to do with the Lord and were in the Church only to shatter it from within. Therefore, launching manifold discussions without substance is only an excuse for people pretending to have a divergence of opinion. Whereas, in reality, they all are of the same faction and cunningly advance their evil plot. We are living 2 Peter 2:1–2: *". . . false prophets also arose among the people, just as there will be false teachers among you, who will secretly bring in destructive heresies, even denying the Master who bought them, bringing upon themselves swift destruction. And many will follow their sensuality, and because of them the way of truth will be blasphemed."* (ESV)

Throughout history, many have considered the apocrypha as not eligible for the Church's teachings, but only for the private interest of the reader. Since when do earthly considerations supersede the quest of eternal life? The fact that they recognize it's not fitting for the public already states such writings have nothing to do with God's knowledge and, thus, should be discarded. Hebrews 13:9 reads, *"Do not be led away by diverse and strange teachings, for it is good for the heart to be strengthened by grace, not by foods, which have not benefited those devoted to them."*

(ESV)

Advising anyone to read these books is simply to waste such one's precious time. On the contrary, that time should be wisely used in studying scriptures that bring the mind of the Lord. Because only such teachings will save one's soul at the end, when challenged in the day of evil.

When decisions were made in the past to exclude books currently in the New Testament, other than Matthew, it's evident those making the decisions had a perspective dissimilar from the Lord's. How could one question the book of Revelation, for example? Either because such people want to prevent the public from being enlightened, or they have carnal minds, which can't perceive God's wisdom. Unfortunately, the Church possesses both disadvantages in these end times and surely always have. Because we are the replacement of these evil spirits in the heavenly realm, as future dominions, powers, and authorities, they'll certainly not allow us an easy victory. They will cunningly undermine our progress until the end, though we all know they are already defeated: Christ is at the right hand of the Father and has received all power on earth and heaven. Thus, it's just a matter a time, which they use well.

Faith without deeds is dead. Some have questioned the book of James because of its focus on deeds rather than faith, yet his admonition is to make our faith alive through our works, linking Moses's law to Jesus' love. Hence the words of the apostle Paul in Romans 3:31. *"Do we then overthrow the law by this faith? By no means! On the contrary, we uphold the law."* (ESV)

Wherefore, the apostle John rightly exposes such reality when in his exhortation, he inquires with his first letter in verses 3:17–18, *". . . if anyone has the world's goods and sees his brother in need, yet closes his heart against him, how does God's love abide in him? Little children, let us not love in word or talk but in deed and in truth."* (ESV)

As apocrypha's first meaning defined book that conveyed esoteric knowledge, which was hidden from general audience, as not initiated, these were therefore exchanged in secret. Since esoterism has all to do with magic, even sorcery, which means witchcraft, isn't it the Matthew story aligning with that perspective? Seeing the deliberate intention to discredit the Lord's teachings, by targeting its foundational doctrines, and teaching its opposite as being the truth? One could think an anonymous wanted to leave his mark on history and wrote that novel, which became popular through circumstance. However, when you notice two nearly identical previous versions of that story already existed, what was the need to add a third one, and how could the Church leaders accept it and disregard its various discrepancies? And above all this, place it as the forefront of the New Testament?

The book of Matthew performs several evil deceptions: It discourages true believers by crushing their faith and casting away those who were still hesitating. Meanwhile, it convinces evildoers and other students of the devil that the main character in the story is actually a deceiver who has managed to fool a crowd without being caught. But if this is the case, how is it that all evil spirits are cast out simply by the authority of His name? How is it that people are set free and others are healed in the name of Jesus Christ? If He were a usurper, would His followers willingly accept being killed, knowing that it is all a fraud? Would He be able to conquer death and appear to many at the same time to prove the resurrection? Even the Pharisees ask an interesting question in John 9:16. *"Some of the Pharisees said, "This man is not from God, because he does not keep the Sabbath. But others said, "How can a man who is a sinner perform such signs?" And there was division among them."* (ESV)

And even among the Jews, the same query remained in John 10:19-21. *"Again there was division among the Jews because of these words. Many of them said, "He has a demon and is insane; why listen to him?" Others said, "These are not the words of one who is oppressed by a demon. Can a demon open the eyes of the blind?"* (ESV)

There is one certainty about the ministry of Jesus Christ of Nazareth, and that is the works He performed were unseen, and to this day only His followers have been able to reproduce such miracles. Wizards and magicians are not able to do the same for the simple reason that God the Father doesn't allow it, because it would cause confusion, and on the other hand, the devil never releases his prisoners. Christians are far more powerful than sorcerers, but most of them just don't know it. ——*"My people are destroyed for lack of knowledge . . ."* (NKJV) (Hosea 4:6) Just as angels are mightier than fallen angels—known as demons, because angels are led by the Holy Spirit of God and carry His authority. Similarly, are miracles done by Christians through the Holy Spirit.

The Antichrist, however, will do mighty works because he will be allowed to condemn those who delight in sin and refuse to change their ways of hatred, as the apostle Paul explains in 2 Thessalonians 2:9-12. *"The coming of the lawless one is by the activity of Satan with all power and false signs and wonders, and with all wicked deception for those who are perishing, because they refused to love the truth and so be saved. Therefore God sends them a strong delusion, so that they may believe what is false, in order that all may be condemned who did not believe the truth but had pleasure in unrighteousness."* (ESV)

We can see that God will allow the devil to accomplish a task, just as He did with Job. Only this time, unlike Job's case, the victims will be condemned to eternal damnation because the centuries of warnings never cause them to reflect on their evil deeds, to change their behavior. The false prophet will then be sent to encapsulate the fate of such people.

Obviously, someone hasn't done its homework, to have the Godhead recognized as a single entity centuries after many apostles unmistakably proved that evidence. Manifold other debates of the Church's leaders demonstrate an obvious departure from the communion with the Holy Spirit, to dive in philosophy. All their alleged debates around established doctrines are nothing but a smoke that purposely creates a foggy situation, allowing them, through endless arguments, to converge toward a preestablished objective. If apostles have established without the shadow of a doubt, and even Jewish High priests had the Lord crucified, because they consider it a blasphemy that Christ declared to be the Son of God; if then the Lord's Divine nature is established as His condemnation to death sentence, how come such discussion arises later in different councils? Just as it's done with the story of Matthew, which author is often depicted as one making errors because he knew very little about Jewish customs, and based his work on an obsolete version of the Bible: Deceivers need to create chaos, an ambiguous setting where their mischiefs will be implemented without drawing attention. With disorder, it's easier to start some events creating a diversion that will entertain while the implementation of the hidden plan is made. Such procedure is still done regularly in politics: Laws often adopted in times of crises show that pattern, if they are even noticed in the first place. Likewise, there are often odd events around presidential elections, which are often seen as the machinations of a candidate's opposite camp. In reality, it's simply a distraction to draw attention to something meaningless while a deception is implemented; just as prestidigitation is a set of tricks that confuse the mind, preventing witnesses from seeing what's being done. All these maneuvers fall under one single umbrella labeled lie. Any of its kind is of the devil.

When scanning the Church's history, it's evident wolves appeared very early in its midst and caused drastic damage by corrupting it from the top to the bottom. The apostle John's letter already shows that tendency, in 3 John 1:9–10. *"I wrote to the church, but Diotrephes, who loves to have the preeminence among them, does not receive us. Therefore, if I come, I will call to mind his deeds which he does, prating against us with malicious words. And not content with that, he himself does not receive the brethren, and forbids those who wish to, putting them out of the church."* (NKJV)

The strategy is designed to drain the Church and expel all its true believers—those who focus on helping others aren't obsessed by their status within the congregation. But as wolves have a carnal mind, thus only consider earthly matters, obtaining that position of leadership is earnestly coveted. This was already the case with leaders in the time preceding the Lord's advent, as endeavoring to always be and, regrettably, achieving to often stay at the top of any hierarchy, as Micah prophesied in 3:9–10: *"Now hear this, you heads of the house of Jacob And rulers of the house of Israel, Who abhor justice And pervert all equity, Who build Zion with bloodshed And Jerusalem with iniquity."* (NKJV)

We can see from the first part of that scripture, the whole headship has been greatly corrupted by evil practices, only to satisfy their cupidity. In verse 11, the prophet clearly exposes the wrongdoings of these leaders of the Jewish kingdom. *"Her heads judge for a bribe, Her priests teach for pay, And her prophets divine for money. Yet they lean on the LORD, and say, 'Is not the LORD among us? No harm can come upon us.'"* (NKJV)

If, at some point in history, the scandalous drifting of the Church's leaders brought the reformation, it only proves they could no longer restrain people's growing anger in view of their obvious pagan values. One appointed as its leader only brought something seemingly different in appearances, however the mindset is the same. Thus, Protestantism has become a good image of that result, with the multifarious denominations having each one a particular way to see and understand the Holy Word of God.

The apostles' experience shows, however, that the Holy Spirit always guides in cohesion and harmony. Thus, when Paul meets Peter, John and James to expound what he teaches the Gentiles, it corresponds perfectly to the doctrine they received from the Lord during His ministry, although Paul received it by revelation (having never met the Lord before His crucifixion), and they received it by direct teaching, as written in Galatians 2:9. *"and when James, Cephas, and John, who seemed to be pillars, perceived the grace that had been given to me, they gave me and Barnabas the right hand of fellowship, that we should go to the Gentiles and they to the circumcised."* (NKJV)

Similarly, when Apollos is noticed by Aquilas, it's clear that the Holy Spirit is guiding his approach, even though he only knew the baptism of John at the time of the event, according to Acts 18:25. *"He had been instructed in the way of the Lord. And being fervent in spirit, he spoke and taught accurately the things concerning Jesus, though he knew only the baptism of John."* (ESV) And he would later become a faithful collaborator of the apostle Paul.

What, on the other hand, is demonstrated by the various diversifications of the church, is only the errancy in philosophy and a complete abandonment of the truth of God by His Holy Spirit. Catholicism, though seemingly organized with a head that's followed regardless of its eccentricities, is likewise plunged in the darkness of this world's pursuit. Wealth and power are what they all chase, and their audience simply serves as a means to achieve that goal. What happened in Eden is what we are living in the Church nowadays. As it has been back then, the same cause will produce an identical result: a purge will cleanse it of all its defects.

Yet as always in time past, in the various epochs of scandals, there has been a remnant of faithful believers. All are thoroughly persecuted and hindered in so many ways, history itself proves their voices couldn't be heard by the public, for they were smothered by the "legends faction's" deafening clamor with its various defamation campaigns. Surely noise takes one's attention from what is observed, to eventually suppress it through diverse machinations while the subject is entertained. It is written in Psalms 44:22. *"Yet for Your sake we are killed all day long; We are accounted as sheep for the slaughter."* (NKJV) Our rights are openly contravened day after day, and we are deprived of everything we ever believe to possess. Our last rampart is the Bible, and yet it has been defiled by apocrypha accounts inserted as legitimate, thus canonized.

It's certain that a Christian is considered a rogue individual on this earth, since such is against its system based on lies through legends, and therefore fantasy. Because of his belief in the truth and obedience to the Lord Jesus Christ and not the various entities disseminated by the devil, such a person is seen as the enemy. Surely a believer and therefore disciple of the Lord Jesus Christ is led by virtues and not perversion, which abounds in this world and leads all who've pledged allegiance to that culture. Since Christians' King and highest authority differs from that of this world, there are conflicts of interest: A Christian has all his expectations set on the next span, even life eternal in heaven, while others have no expectations after this life. When therefore, the latter strive to manifest a meaningful treasure of wealth on earth, such is meaningless for the follower of Jesus. He will acquire everything and does not need to chase what is already his inheritance. Because all things work together for good in his life, such one is certain to achieve what God wants him to manifest on earth.

Since God's mind is obtained through the Bible, which has been corrupted, it's only a proof that validates what has been foretold and demonstrates the prominence of the knowledge imparted to us by the Lord. If often scorned and turned in derision, history and these facts around Christians' reality attest all is done to discourage a community that's too powerful to be left in complete autonomy. Such would counterfeit the whole scheme of this world with implementation of values that dismantle mischiefs on which this society is grounded.

One may inquire: but where is God in all this turmoil? Why doesn't He intervene? What we are living has been foretold, and history is following a predicted path: there's nothing new or changed in the announced plan. Thus, if God guides His children to save their souls, the mischievous are just digging the hole in which they'll all be laid. The chaos they create forces the uprights to adopt a particular behavior, which opposes the world's conduct and creates a conflict that requires choosing between these two contradictory perspectives: God's or the world's. Christians must realize that being a disciple of Jesus Christ means to be part of a special unit in the army of the living God, specially trained in the fierceness of adversity to become like our Lord, as the apostle Paul said in Romans 8:16-17. *"The Spirit himself bears witness with our spirit that we are children of God, and if children, then heirs—heirs of God and fellow heirs with Christ, provided we suffer with him in order that we may also be glorified with him."* (ESV) Moreover, he adds in 2 Timothy 2:3-5. *"You therefore must endure hardship as a good soldier of Jesus Christ. No one engaged in warfare entangles himself with the affairs of this life, that he may please him who enlisted him as a soldier. And also if anyone competes in athletics, he is not crowned unless he competes according to the rules."* (NKJV)

We are ushered on this road leading to Armageddon, and we'll encounter more and more troubles as time goes by. The Lord said we must not be troubled by them, thus we must focus on keeping His commandments until the end, regardless of the fierceness of the adversity we'll face. If in this world soldiers prove their talents by their ability to convey violence, in the army of the living God, our skills are demonstrated by the aptitude we have to keep our composure and live in peace with our surroundings, regardless of their conduct toward us. At all costs, we must remain calm and confident: The Lord is fully in control of all things and teaches us through a tough and yet meaningful experience, the values of an unshakable Kingdom we will inherit and lead with Him.

Knowing most of the Church leaders, after the apostolic era were increasingly corrupted, conscious likewise of the harmfulness of fantasies in a believer's faith—teaching lies contradicting faith facts, thus imparting doubts, it's wise not to dive in the apocryphal section of any kind. That venture can only be harmful for such believers' faith. Either esoteric matters will be encountered or cunningly designed deceits will be faced, both crafted to hurt whoever dares to take a sneak peek. One must always remember, the devil has designed all these deceptions simply to trap people in a mind prison: the worst one can be stuck into, because it has no physical bars and walls that can be demolished, but lies that control how one's mind functions. Thus, it makes that person the prey of every other deceit the devil designed to keep manhood in bondage under his wicked ruling, therefore such prey becoming his follower.

The Church is in a constant purge of its true believers, by foes who cunningly persecute them through numerous stratagems, of which witchcraft plays a preponderant role. It's common to experience all sorts of calamities once joining a new congregation, varying from financial blows to spiritual attacks, like strange dreams with that clearly evil connotation, the most prevalent disaster being strife in the household. If the works of the flesh are the expression of carnal minds, they strive to transmit them into the lives of righteous people, with devastating consequences, as Mark says in 7:22-23. *". . . evil thoughts, adulteries, fornications, murders, thefts, covetousness, wickedness, deceit, lewdness, an evil eye, blasphemy, pride, foolishness. All these evil things come from within and defile a man."* (ESV)

Through various means, these uprights are enticed to walk in a way that opposes the law of God, which is love. Surely perverting members had been observed as early as the Lord's ministry, when the Pharisees, Sadducees, and Herodians tried to make Him follow their customs, which the Lord clearly denounced by exposing their hypocrisy, as described in Luke 11:39-42. "*. . . the Lord said to him, "Now you Pharisees clean the outside of the cup and of the dish; but your inside is full of greed and wickedness. You foolish ones, did He who made the outside not make the inside also? But give that which is within as a charitable gift, and then all things are clean for you. "But woe to you Pharisees! For you pay tithes of mint, rue, and every kind of garden herb, and yet you ignore justice and the love of God; but these are the things you should have done without neglecting the others."* (NASB)

Such maneuvering only increased in apostolic ministries, as it's reported in Galatians 2:3–5. "*Yet not even Titus who was with me, being a Greek, was compelled to be circumcised. And this occurred because of false brethren secretly brought in (who came in by stealth to spy out our liberty which we have in Christ Jesus, that they might bring us into bondage), to whom we did not yield submission even for an hour, that the truth of the gospel might continue with you."* (NKJV)

Surely, these uprights will be allured by various persons and means, concealing thereby their threats' sources. Chaos will often prompt believers to seek advice from unfortunately, the very ones who launched these evil machinations in one's life: leaders of a devil's church, labeled in the book of Revelation 3:9 as "*Synagogue of Satan*" by the Lord.

How could one distinguish such entities to avoid being one of their preys? Reading the Bible which is learning the truth that sets one free is the only way out of that situation. "*So if the Son sets you free, you will be free indeed."* (ESV) (John 8:36)

Not only do these wolves work at removing true believers, but their plan is backed by that deception introduced in the Bible as being books inspired by the Lord, namely Matthew, Esther, and Song of Songs by Solomon. And to make it even worse—because uprights' numerous schisms could bring about a real Church that would bring back to life the heritage of the apostles, which has been corrupted—false leaders were erected to offer a deceptive solution to what has become unbearable for many believers. But when observing the

Lutheran church, one may wonder if the Lord ever used people who were tormented, as such a leader is often depicted by various historians. It never has been the way God has operated throughout the long history of His people. If that personage is widely attributed to the movement of reformation—which is debatable, but won't be done here—the outcome of such a venture proves it was a way to trap these true believers who oppose the clergy's anarchy, and seek a meaningful institution that properly represents the virtues of the only true God, by righteousness, justice, and an abode in sanctification. So the Jewish root was split in two, and Christians took their own path, only to be divided into factions that unfortunately for most of them, seek only earthly rewards: The same cause is producing a similar effect throughout history. Consequently, truthful churches with Christ Jesus' values are drawn in an ocean of entities proceeding from the devil, and whose network is very active and communicates abundantly in deceits, hiding thereby attempts of true worshipers to speak out.

What option remains for the real believer in this end times, with a Church that has been corrupted in all aspects of its structure? Catholics, like Protestants, are perverted and aim for earthly gains, discarding what makes the strength of Christianity: love through the Holy Spirit. Surely one who hasn't the Spirit of Jesus doesn't belong to Him, which the conduct of most of these "be leavers" prove with their ostensible expression of an utmost carnal mind. In Eden, the serpent seduced Eve and corrupted her mind through lies. Adam and her trusted a fantasy to be the truth and vice versa. Israelites had a similar status of holiness when they engaged in sexual immorality, followed by being idolatrous with Moabite women. Men consequently bowing before their idols led Israel to yoke itself to Baal Peor, the gods they went to worship. Since Christians can't be challenged on the grounds of power—being of God Almighty, because of their absolute supremacy, made by their fellowship in Holiness with the Holy God's Spirit, making them vulnerable through the separation from their strength, by enticing them to abandon the law of God is the strategy used, just like in time past. Mixing pagan cultures with Christianity is like trying to blend love and hatred. Inevitably, love will fly away: it can't stand lawlessness. It's like mixing clear water with filthy water. That mixture becomes soiled. Though it appears clearer than its unclean original source, it remains dirty. If Christianity is mixed with paganism, it's simply a pagan ritual with a tint of Christianity, but God isn't in that and, as such, can't save a soul from His coming wrath.

What then must one do who wants to live the real faith in the Lord Jesus if most congregations no longer provide the knowledge needed, but mostly teach philosophy instead? Reading the Bible remains the foremost way to grow in the Lord Jesus' knowledge. Just as those in Beret checked that the teaching was correct, so too must any faithful believer who wants to avoid the pitfalls of false doctrines. Acts 17:11 reports that: *"These were more fair-minded than those in Thessalonica, in that they received the word with all readiness, and searched the Scriptures daily to find out whether these things were so."* (NKJV)

Seeking for the truth and praying to God to impart His Holy Spirit's acumen is the starting point. It's written in John 16:13, *"When the Spirit of truth comes, he will guide you into all the truth, . . ."* (ESV)

James corroborated that principle of the Holy Spirit giving wisdom in his exhortation's outline, by stating in 1:5, *"If any of you lacks wisdom, let him ask God, who gives generously to all without reproach, and it will be given him."* (ESV)

That assertion confirms what Luke wrote in his account, after the Lord explained to His disciples in Luke 11:9, we must ask and it will be given to us; seek and we'll find; knock and it will be opened to us. Verses 11:11–13 read, *"If a son asks for bread from any father among you, will he give him a stone? Or if he asks for a fish, will he give him a serpent instead of a fish? Or if he asks for an egg, will he offer him a scorpion? If you then, being evil, know how to give good gifts to your children, how much more will your heavenly Father give the Holy Spirit to those who ask Him!"* (NKJV)

Acquiring a good knowledge of God allows to spot false teachings, as well as become a worthy resource for that congregation. Moreover, we can only impact others and save our souls by walking as per the Lord's teaching, as written in 1 Timothy 4:16. *"Pay close attention to yourself and to the teaching; persevere in these things, for as you do this you will save both yourself and those who hear you."* (NASB)

If mainstream methods are clogged, the Lord's compassion made the Bible available for all, with its study accessible to all believers. The more one reads, and more will such become used to Bible's expressions and allegories. Then as one explanation leads to another, awareness just keeps expanding. In Proverbs 25:2 we are reminded of the following truth, which must always be at the forefront of our study. *"It is the glory of God to conceal a matter, But the glory of kings is to search out a matter."* (NKJV)

Anyone who is willing to know the truth of God can become erudite and grow far above many who are seen as great teachers, but are in reality sorcerers teaching philosophy, thus acclaimed by the world. God has no pleasure in such people, and they'll be disappointed before the Throne of Grace when receiving their appraisal. Certainly, many of today's first will end up cast out.

A good method for studying the Bible quickly is through an audiobook, a read-aloud option in a word processing software, or simply from a website that offers an audio version for example. The read aloud option is preferred because some audiobooks have subliminal messages to hinder one's understanding of God's Word—whenever music plays in the background of an audiobook's narration, that's a red flag. Unfortunately, this is discovered after one has heard it several times and notices that something odd is happening. Sadly, it's hard to tell nowadays who's trustworthy and which website has a dependable version. One must do one's due diligence here, to investigate the best option available. Certainly, the main outlets seem the safest, as it would be too costly for them to engage in such inappropriate behavior. Howbeit, the harmless way, though most tedious, is to record one own's read aloud on a computer, then listening to the recording either on the computer or downloading it to a mobile device to listen with even more freedom of mobility. This allows to go about normal daily activities while listening to the Bible.

In addition, there are several websites that list numerous versions of the Bible, which are very useful for learning and comparing the translated Scriptures. Not only are these free, but they are also very helpful in assessing which version to use for study, and even comparing them when in doubt about certain passages. They certainly complement the audio, and this combination gives a better understanding of the Scriptures. I would highly recommend them, as I've found so far that all versions are complementary and no one gives a translation that is always the best, and for some the translation can even be simply wrong or misleading. These sites often give the Aramaic, Hebrew and Greek translations as well. This makes it possible to see the literal translation word by word and to understand the true meaning of the Scriptures.

Genesis, the prophets, and the New Testament are undeniably books that give a better understanding and greater insight to a walk in love, per God's commandments. The Psalms are very powerful because they are the prayers of faithful servants of the Lord, so they will uphold any sorrowful heart in distress, and even strengthen and bolster such a heart against spiritual attacks. Reading them out loud when overwhelmed by a situation makes them so much more personal, and creates that communion with the Holy Spirit that helps to express what's in the deepest parts of the heart. It's crucial to understand that these are NOT magic formulas, but rather good examples to follow when expressing deep feelings. They can be used to start the conversation with God, and then continue with more personal words. The more sincere and unpretentious our heart is before the Lord, the closer and stronger our communion with the Holy Spirit becomes. The Proverbs, on the other hand, give a good understanding of what righteousness is. It's a good habit to take notes, write down questions that arise, and try to find the answer in what has been told. These notes will become very precious, as they will trace one's reasoning and progress in the understanding of Jesus. It's written in John 14:26, *"But the Helper, the Holy Spirit, whom the Father will send in My name, He will teach you all things, and bring to your remembrance all things that I said to you."* (NKJV)

To remember something, it's needed to have been heard or read first. Being acquainted with God's Holy Word can only better one's understanding of life in general while brightening hopes by changing the paradigm. Since God created the world, wouldn't learning from the manual He sent for its effective use benefit all those who are involved?

The Bible—apart from Matthew, Esther, and Song of Songs—possesses everything a Christian needs to save his soul, walk in love per God's standard, and influence people by establishing the example for the group. Its teachings are comprehensive and need no addition. What's found in it can be verified by historic sources, as it's based on truth, thus tangible facts. It's conceived in a way that allows one to continuously grow in its knowledge without needing to get another book. As knowledge expands, the scholar likewise keeps discovering even greater truths and meaning disseminated throughout its various chronicles. With it, the discovery never ceases, and there is always something new.

The world is literally changed when observing it through God's insight: It becomes the reality.

6 INTRUSION

The book of Esther doesn't mention God, not even once. Nor does it teach to rely on Him. Rather, it's more about human traditions without any grounds in God's Word, not even the Lord's Wisdom but only those of men. Yet Ezekiel's prophecy concerning God's people tells us we should not live as per the traditions of man, but upon God's precepts of righteousness. It's written in 20:18, *"And I said to their children in the wilderness, 'Do not walk in the statutes of your fathers, nor keep their rules, nor defile yourselves with their idols. I am the Lord your God; walk in my statutes, and be careful to obey my rules,'"* (ESV)

The apostle John tells of the Lord's criticism of the Jews who expected to find life eternal in the scrolls in 5:39: *"You search the Scriptures because you think that in them you have eternal life; and it is they that bear witness about me."* (ESV)

Psalms 40:6–7 reads, *"Sacrifice and offering You did not desire; My ears You have opened. Burnt offering and sin offering You did not require. Then I said, 'Behold, I come; In the scroll of the book it is written of me."* (ESV)

Take note that this scripture has been wrongly translated in many Bible versions, though that same scripture is also written by a Jewish author of the apostolic time, therefore rendering what was transcribed in Hebrew and clarifying it in a Greek letter. It's written in Hebrews 10:5–7, *"Consequently, when Christ came into the world, he said, 'Sacrifices and offerings you have not desired, but a body have you prepared for me; in burnt offerings and sin offerings you have taken no pleasure.' Then I said, 'Behold, I have come to do your will, O God, as it is written of me in the scroll of the book.'"* (ESV)

Assuredly, if the Hebrews' epistle isn't from Paul, as diverse remarks of Church leaders from the postapostolic ministries determined to justify its initial rejection from the collection of the Bible's books, that epistle is nonetheless from a distinguished servant of the Lord. That letter's formulation and the methodology used to communicate its knowledge, even the vocabulary, is reminiscent of the apostle Paul. Could it be another deceit? No! First of all, the acumen found in that letter to the Hebrews is in complete resonance with the rest of the Bible's truthful books and even sheds light on some points partially explained elsewhere. Why such resemblance then in its context and ideas? Luke gives an explanation clarifying the mystery in Acts 18:1–5: *"After this Paul left Athens and went to Corinth. And he found a Jew named Aquila, a native of Pontus, recently come from Italy with his wife Priscilla, because Claudius had commanded all the Jews to leave Rome. And he went to see them, and because he was of the same trade he stayed with them and worked, for they were tentmakers by trade. And he reasoned in the synagogue every Sabbath, and tried to persuade Jews and Greeks. When Silas and Timothy arrived from Macedonia, Paul was occupied with the word, testifying to the Jews that the Christ was Jesus."* (ESV)

Paul lived in Aquila's house and worked with him. Aquila experienced the various tribulations the apostle went through, and even helped him at the peril of their lives, to foster the revelation of God's Word, as Paul recalled in his letter to the Romans in 16:3. *"Greet Prisca and Aquila, my fellow workers in Christ Jesus, who risked their necks for my life, to whom not only I give thanks but all the churches of the Gentiles give thanks as well."* (ESV)

The epistle can't be from Timothy, who was also with Paul for a long season, because the ending clearly states he was released, thus the author knew him very well and even adds a mention confirming it's Aquila's, as reads Hebrews 13:23–24: *"You should know that our brother Timothy has been released, with whom I shall see you if he comes soon. Greet all your leaders and all the saints. Those who come from Italy send you greetings."* (ESV)

Aquila lived in Italy and logically conveyed messages from those who had been there and brought him news. It couldn't be Titus either since he's not a Jew, as the introduction of the epistle stipulates in its very first verse, as written in Hebrews 1:1: *"Long ago, at many times and in many ways, God spoke to our fathers by the prophets."* (ESV)

All the evidence points to Aquilas, who, as the Apostle Paul mentions in his letter, is a minister of the church in his house. His explanations and the rhetoric he uses are of a preacher, a teacher of the law of God. Though it's close to Paul's teachings, it shows in some aspect to have a less potent unction, though still very abundant and shrewd. That letter enlightens the path of righteousness and corroborates what the walk in love through Jesus means.

The whole Bible is about God saving mankind by His Word; that is, Jesus Christ, the Lord and only Way for life eternal. Fasting isn't observed only by God's people and cannot by itself demonstrate that one abides in Him. Many Jews had gone astray and worshipped idols. The simple fact that the whole book of Esther doesn't contain even a mention, quote, or teaching of God's principles raises doubts of the legitimacy of it being added as a canon in the Bible. From Genesis to Revelation, the Lord God teaches through the story of His people what principles must be held by anyone seeking to serve Him and be His child.

It's written in Isaiah 56:1–7, *"Thus says the LORD: 'Keep justice, and do righteousness, for soon my salvation will come, and my deliverance be revealed. Blessed is the man who does this, and the son of man who holds it fast, who keeps the Sabbath, not profaning it, and keeps his hand from doing any evil.' Let not the foreigner who has joined himself to the LORD say, 'The LORD will surely separate me from his people'; and let not the eunuch say, 'Behold, I am a dry tree.' For thus says the LORD: 'To the eunuchs who keep my Sabbaths, who choose the things that please me and hold fast my covenant, I will give in my house and within my walls a monument and a name better than sons and daughters; I will give them an everlasting name that shall not be cut off. And the foreigners who join themselves to the LORD, to minister to him, to love the name of the LORD, and to be his servants, everyone who keeps the Sabbath and does not profane it, and holds fast my covenant—these I will bring to my holy mountain, and make them joyful in my house of prayer; their burnt offerings and their sacrifices will be accepted on my altar; for my house shall be called a house of prayer for all peoples.'"* (ESV)

In all times, Israel has integrated strangers in its midst, as it was throughout Jacob's route from Paddan-Aram to the house of his father, Isaac, in Canaan, like when they left Egypt and even when they entered the promised land. These were invited to follow their religious customs to be seen as Israelites, as Ezekiel 47:21–23 reports: *"So you shall divide this land among you according to the tribes of Israel. You shall allot it as an inheritance for yourselves and for the sojourners who reside among you and have had children among you. They shall be to you as native-born children of Israel. With you they shall be allotted an inheritance among the tribes of Israel. In whatever tribe the sojourner resides, there you shall assign him his inheritance, declares the Lord God."* (ESV)

The story of Esther is that of a pagan king using the kingdom's virgins as a harem to designate his next queen. If the triviality of that circumstance already sets a precedent in the Bible, the downfall of that tragedy is to see a Jew who's not forced to comply, sending his orphan niece he's raising as his own child to fulfill that mockery and consequently acquire a status of favored in a foreign country. Has prostitution ever been a virtue upheld in the whole Word of God or in any of His teachings? Hasn't He commanded stoning people who have that demeanor? Yet such is here presented as something normal; here is one who will be presented as being of great reputation and very influential, working for the prosperity of his people. But then, what kind of influence would such individual have? Surely, a procurer is highly regarded in his sphere of influence. Does it mean they are recommendable? Is it such an example that one seeking to walk in God's path of righteousness must follow? What insight exactly does the conduct of Mordecai bring in the whole story of Esther? What if the king didn't want her after approaching her? Would that have been a valid reason to lose her virginity? An attempt to enter the king's palace? Isn't prostitution based on the very same principle? How are regarded women acting as such?

In that story, favoritism is apparent by the eunuch who advises only Esther but not the remaining virgins. Why should such favoritism be seen as normal? Injustice is unfair, regardless of the subject. Likewise, an emphasis is placed on the Jewish people's reputation without any grounds for it, like it's also made to present Mordecai as some influential individual before the king. There's no grounds on which these affirmations are based; neither are they references that would justify such prestige. Moreover, the queen Esther asks to fast for three days. Interestingly, there is no mention about making petition to God for the situation to be resolved. What's the purpose of the fast then? Daniel, who prayed with his friends in Babylon, invited them to join him to understand the king's dream in Daniel 2:17–18: "*Then Daniel went to his house and made the matter known to Hananiah, Mishael, and Azariah, his companions, and told them to seek mercy from the God of heaven concerning this mystery, so that Daniel and his companions might not be destroyed with the rest of the wise men of Babylon.*" (ESV)

There is no mention made to which divinity the fast is presented to obtain favor before the king or when she will enter the court without being invited and, thus, avoid the death sentence if he feels offended. Even the reply of Mordecai, who's supposed to be full of wisdom, established before the king as his first counselor and growing in influence within the king's court, doesn't demonstrate such prevalence. The king is invited to a feast, and the queen Esther requests her people to be spared, which is granted. The king then allows Mordecai and Esther to write whatever they wish, to overrule what had been written previously. This ostensible absence of the king's authority—having foreigners decide the kingdom's fate on his behalf—is highly questionable. And when this has been done, with casualties reported to the king, the queen asks for yet a second round. That whole story just doesn't align with anything else throughout the whole Bible, other than accounts like Matthew and Song of Songs. Many details in that story don't fit with God's teachings and knowledge. It has no insight into or instruction about ways to better our lives, which can be found in seemingly akin stories like Ruth. On top of that, the only reference made to set its authenticity refers to writings outside the Bible, and moreover of pagans, as Esther 10:2 reads, *"And all the acts of his power and might, and the full account of the high honor of Mordecai, to which the king advanced him, are they not written in the Book of the Chronicles of the kings of Media and Persia?"* (ESV)

Since when does the Lord's scripture refer to an external source? One that's not only foreign in customs and religious beliefs but has nothing to do with the soul's salvation? Should then Christians seek references in their religion? We can see once again the cunning work of the antichrist. That sentence uses the same terms as those found in the books of Chronicles and Kings. However, it is misleading because it gives an impression of déjà vu, but the reference mentioned in this case is different. Thus, the ending is twisted to deceive the reader. No wonder that not even one reference to the Most High God is made throughout that story of Esther. It should be instead labeled and seen as literature for Media and Persia, but not placed in the Hebrew Bible. God is Holy, which means truth prevails always in all of His realizations.

Esther's account has many similarities with the story of Joseph in Egypt, which is found earlier in the Bible. Thus, it should resonate somehow in the reader's mind and bring a compelling feeling to this account that will unconsciously instill trust. The last verse of that story explains Mordecai's role and influence in the kingdom. However, it clearly states that it's only for his people, whereas Joseph in Egypt was an example for all communities. Pharaoh himself established the people of God in the best region of the land for a reason: Joseph saved that land from a catastrophic drought and held the solution that saved these people. Besides, God allowing only Joseph to explain dreams that Pharaoh's multifarious sorcerers and magicians could not, proved to his master that God was with him, and consequently his name was changed to the Egyptian one of Zaphenath-paneah, which when translated means "the God speaks and He lives." Joseph demonstrated his virtues and abilities throughout his experiences in his first master's house, where he grew in respectability in the eyes of that Egyptian because God was with him. Then while in prison, alike state of God's grace prevailed and finally as being the lord of that dominion, ruling beside Pharaoh. The procession that went up in Canaan to bury Joseph's father in the cave that's in the field at Machpelah, to the east of Mamre, attests to his reputation and dignity held before the Egyptians, as tells Genesis 50:7: *"So Joseph went up to bury his father. With him went up all the servants of Pharaoh, the elders of his household, and all the elders of the land of Egypt."* (ESV)

Interestingly, the story of Esther follows the pattern seen in Joseph's story, removing all references to the Lord. Mordecai is the first before the king, like Joseph was in Egypt; he allowed his community to be spared from a horrifying massacre, while Joseph saved the entire region around Upper and Lower Egypt from seven years of famine. Esther is an orphan while Joseph is kind of an orphan: His mother is deceased and he is sold as a slave, taken from his loving father and the rest of the family. Surely, pushing the emotional buttons in people's minds leads them to overlook various aspects of that account, which is a way for adversaries to imperceptibly corrupt readers' perceptions, and bring about a reality that's only confusing. Such will never be God's plan, nor can it be something that brings salvation but only death.

Our identity in the Almighty and Holy Living God not only prevents such derision, but our status as the sons of the true and only God Creator of all things gives us an assurance that transcends the meaningless things of this world. We need not to boast and lie about our history, for it is full of wonders from the Almighty and contains real facts. We have no need to try embellishing the reality; it's already amazing beyond acknowledgment. Thus, walking in truth and justice is how we distinguish ourselves from those whose names aren't in the book of life.

7 INANITY

What is the purpose of Solomon's Song of Songs in the midst of these Bible scrolls? The whole Word of God is about Jesus Christ as the Way of truth to return to love: God's ministry, not mankind's affection, though it's permitted with a full and exhaustive law. God's Word is only about Salvation, as it was rightly said by the Lord in Hebrews 10:7, reiterating what was said in the prophecy illustrated in Psalms 40:7: *"Then I said, 'Behold, I have come to do your will, O God, as it is written of me in the scroll of the book.'"* (ESV)

Whenever intimacy is depicted in the whole Bible, it's always in a very gracious way: A man approaches his woman, or knows his wife, or even as Leviticus admonishes not to uncover the nakedness. The prophet Isaiah expresses it in 8:3, *"And I went to the prophetess, and she conceived and bore a son. . ."* (ESV)

In the book of Proverbs, the Lord recommends always being enamored of your wife as we read in verses 5:18-19. *"Let your fountain be blessed, and rejoice in the wife of your youth, a lovely deer, a graceful doe. Let her breasts fill you at all times with delight; be intoxicated always in her love."* (ESV)

The preceding verses also speak of the couple's intimacy,

but again in very gracious terms, in 5:15-17. *"Drink water from your own cistern, flowing water from your own well. Should your springs be scattered abroad, streams of water in the streets? Let them be for yourself alone, and not for strangers with you."* (ESV)

We see that it is advised to avoid sexual immorality advocating multiple partners, but always in a tone that is appropriate for the teaching of virtues and morals.

Regrettably, the Song of Songs relates in so many discernible details what shouldn't be in a collection of Holy books. If, for example, the apostle Paul advises spouses to separate to devote time to prayer and fasting, it clearly shows the couple's intimacy is not compatible with God's Holiness, because such is from the flesh while God's communion is spiritual. They are opposed and therefore abiding in one draws from the other.

If intimacy is allowed in the marriage, its misuse leads to the flesh's works listed in Galatians 5:19–21. *". . . sexual immorality, impurity, sensuality, idolatry, sorcery, enmity, strife, jealousy, fits of anger, rivalries, dissensions, divisions, envy, drunkenness, orgies, and things like these. . ."* (ESV)

Indeed, couples are recommended not to deprive themselves, as the apostle Paul advises in his first letter to the Corinthians in verse 7:3-5. *"The husband should give to his wife her conjugal rights, and likewise the wife to her husband. For the wife does not have authority over her own body, but the husband does. Likewise the husband does not have authority over his own body, but the wife does. Do not deprive one another, except perhaps by agreement for a limited time, that you may devote yourselves to prayer; but then come together again, so that Satan may not tempt you because of your lack of self-control."* (ESV)

However, the previous verses demonstrate why such is a privilege for those who are married. *"Now concerning the things of which you wrote to me: It is good for a man not to touch a woman. Nevertheless, because of sexual immorality, let each man have his own wife, and let each woman have her own husband."* (NKJV) (1 Corinthians 7:1–2)

It's evident the best state of mankind is without physical intimacy, representing the virgins who have always held a predominant place in ministering before the Almighty God. The apostle Paul advises such condition to avoid being distracted while serving the Lord, as it's explained in 1 Corinthians 7:32–35: *"I want you to be free from anxieties. The unmarried man is anxious about the things of the Lord, how to please the Lord. But the married man is anxious about worldly things, how to please his wife, and his interests are divided. And the unmarried or betrothed woman is anxious about the things of the Lord, how to be holy in body and spirit. But the married woman is anxious about worldly things, how to please her husband. I say this for your own benefit, not to lay any restraint upon you, but to promote good order and to secure your undivided devotion to the Lord."* (ESV)

Per the apostle's advice, we can discern it's better to be free from distraction, to be wholly devoted to the Lord. However, as he previously mentioned in verse 7:7, it's not an order but a concession to avoid sexual immorality: *"I wish that all were as I myself am. But each has his own gift from God, one of one kind and one of another."* (ESV)

Naturally, the Lord has disposed some to be married and have descendants like Abraham and his offspring of faithful believers to multiply and populate the world, and some will spend their whole existence only ministering in total independence from any relation. Each of us has his vocation and must act per what has been foreordained. The apostle Paul was single and devoted his entire life after meeting the Lord to serve Him and preach the Most High God's Kingdom through Jesus Christ to the gentiles of neighboring countries. Abraham's descents, having multiplied, constituted the nation of Israel's foundation. Obviously, such people could not remain virgins since God Himself blessed them and said they should be fruitful. We can see it's all about doing what God has ordained and not what mankind wants to do.

When one enters into marriage, his life isn't to spend his

entire time attempting to be fruitful. We bear children to bypass the fatality of death. Thus, becoming one flesh in the offspring allows us to continue God's plan, as it has been with Abraham, for example, or for those upholding similar faith like David and his kin, who ministered the Lord in faith and oversaw His people with a righteous heart. In all situations, God's purpose is what defines the individual's life span and such is what should be exhibited throughout this earthly existence. Therefore, the flesh's works cannot be the most important subject in life, to have an entire book dedicated for its expression; which above this mindlessness, is illustrated in a wording noticeably inappropriate for such publication. Because, it doesn't bring the enlightenment coveted, but on the contrary stirs up the world's lust, which is in complete opposition with everything expressed in that book's various chronicles.

A subtle terminology is held throughout the Bible, especially in the Old Testament, that assembles all the law's teachings, though some versions express a terminology akin to what's decried here. Consequently, everything pertaining to a married couple's intimacy—as it shouldn't exist otherwise—is explained in the books of Moses. Leviticus, in particular, describes how to live in the society. However, this also covers sanitation, medical treatments, and various other subjects of the community's customs. All these subjects are peripherical, while the spiritual enhancement is the main topic. Manhood was created to be temporarily on earth and was never meant to live on it eternally. Therefore, as many have often mentioned, we are pilgrims on earth and must behave as such. This implies that temporary business is of less importance than our eternal endeavor: We are created to serve the Lord Almighty in His tabernacle in Zion, in heavenly realms. Anything else is therefore done to achieve that purpose, be it marrying, bearing children, or learning through the various experiences and tribulations we encounter. Every single thing in our life is made only to establish that reality. Therefore, focusing on one aspect of life that is temporal distracts us from the real purpose of our lives, which is to be trained to serve the Lord as we will do in heaven. Jacob, renamed Israel by God, went to Paddan-Aram to get a woman from Laban's daughters. Misled by his father in-law, he spent twenty years serving there. Though the story depicts an abundant number of wives and concubines, its emphasis is not on the expression of their feelings. Rather, it describes the various aspects of Jacob's life and experience. The king David likewise had manifold wives and concubines, yet his story doesn't reveal such irrelevant elements, not even in the episode with Bathsheba. All the time, a candid yet gracious iteration is reported, which allows the reader to focus on what's essential: growing in the knowledge of the truth by learning through different examples of past stories, God's salvation by His love.

Existence is not about mankind, but God manifesting His love in multifarious ways. When observing nature and especially the beauty it reveals, it voices the Glory of its Creator, be it on earth or in the infinite ends of the interstellar space. Everything declares the Majesty of an Infinite Being, so Holy that He can't be seen with human eyes, but only with the eyes of our heart through love, which can be revealed only in the truth by righteousness.

Solomon's wisdom was given to him by God, but this does not imply that all his writings are included in the Bible. If it is inappropriate, it's because unlike the Proverbs, which are mostly his, the Song of Songs is not intended to elevate the reader's conscience, and therefore doesn't fit in with the rest of the inspired writings.

8 CERTAINTY

The Jewish religious system has been corrupted, leading to the Lord's crucifixion followed by the destruction of the kingdom of Judah. Christianity separated from its Jewish roots to adopt its own identity, amending several teachings of the law. Nevertheless, it became itself alike tarnished thus, brought about the reformation movement. However, unlike both previous partings, the one of the reformation has been orchestrated by the faction producing these turbulences and provided alleged leaders who only established an altered version of the contested religious authority. And even prior to that, as the so-called fathers of the Church became influential and departed from the simplicity of Jesus Christ, to dive in philosophy that led the Church in utmost darkness after the apostolic time, another separation was made that wasn't visible to the naked eye: the spiritual departure from Holiness. Just like it happened with the Jews and the absence of the Ark of the Covenant of the Lord, appearances had replaced the real communion with God. If a replica resembles its original entity, more often than not, it's only in its external appearance. Similarly, though a religious service may seem pious, it's only an orchestration that is played to perfection but without a meaningful aim. The Lord clearly said by Ezekiel in 33:31-32, "... *'they come to you as people do, they sit before you as My people, and they hear your words, but they do not do them; for with their mouth they show much love, but their hearts pursue their own gain. Indeed you are to them as a very lovely song of one who has a pleasant voice and can play well on an instrument; for they hear your words, but they do not do them.'"* (NKJV)

Just like a person not having the Holy Spirit of the Almighty Living God is dead, so much is what represents the various denominations alleging to belong to Jesus, yet denying its Master in every single decision manifested.

The Church moved from Christianity to paganism, conducted by its leaders. The innumerable decisions made throughout history only prove that sad reality: From the various councils' resolutions to the diverse contradictions that the inquisitions illustrate, the evidence of the mind being carnal rather than spiritual is constantly attested. As time goes by, its paganism keeps increasing and its leaders shamelessly and ostensibly reveal more and more the true nature of their faith. Certainly, we're living the end times, and the son of perdition's advent will no longer be delayed. The various considerations permitting such historicity keep surfacing, ratifying past prophecies regarding this season. The son of lawlessness will express the utmost heights of paganism and nonetheless will come from the Church. Therefore, that one must have the various traits that will allow him to pretend to be the real one who was expected, as it's prophesied by Daniel in verses 11:36–37: "*And the king shall do as he wills. He shall exalt himself and magnify himself above every god, and shall speak astonishing things against the God of gods. He shall prosper till the indignation is accomplished; for what is decreed shall be done. He shall pay no attention to the gods of his fathers, or to the one beloved by women. He shall not pay attention to any other god, for he shall magnify himself above all.*" (ESV)

The king will pretend to be God Himself and will do unthinkable things to prove it. Hence, to create the perfect setting for such an event, dispositions are taken and arrangements are made. Therefore, altered, perverted, and corrupted are the various attributes describing nowadays, what the Lord's apostles' legacy has been to mankind. But though it's doleful to see such annihilation, it confirms what has been foretold and announces the renewal of all things. If indeed we are living the preludes of a tempest like no other one, nonetheless, there is always the rainbow after the rainfall.

If the visible part of the Church seems lost in this world's fantasies, a remnant of true believers nonetheless still exists. And if unheard by this world's audience, the eyes and ears of the Lord are very attentive to their petitions. Persecuted in so many ways, they can't even voice their distress; however, such uphold the true worship and the communion with the Holy Spirit. Be it in churches or privately, they continue to perpetrate the traditions once held by the apostles and conveyed to their followers. Such know with certainty the night is coming to its end and the antichrist will be annihilated by the apparition of the Lord Jesus Christ. Therefore, if it's certain we will be confronted by an even greater persecution, the end of these miseries also is nearby. And that end means God's promise of abundance in blissfulness for eternity. The Lord said it plainly in Revelation 22:7 for those keeping His commands, "". . . *behold, I am coming soon. Blessed is the one who keeps the words of the prophecy of this book.*"" (ESV)

Has the Bible been twisted, then? Yes, it has been through history. While the writings themselves, i.e. the accounts of the books that make up the Bible, have not been altered (copies from various sources attest to this), the books of Matthew, Esther and the Song of Songs, nonetheless have been inserted into the canon, to pervert the whole of God's teaching. They have nothing to do with Holiness. Instead of looking for proof that the Word of God has been altered, one must ask why these false accounts were added to the Bible. Because it is proof that this knowledge is too important to be left to Christians alone to use as they see fit. Like Church members were progressively corrupted through generations, so has God's testimony also been tarnished with these teachings that aren't from the Almighty, but from men: Their lack of insight and wisdom clearly demonstrates that state of affairs. And it still is the case nowadays, with various Bible versions offering a translation that's not accurate to the context meant by the original authors. Should people then stop reading the Bible due to such misfortune? No! These attempts to corrupt and therefore misrepresent God's Holy Word don't change His Genuineness. Here is what the apostle Paul said with a similar perspective in Romans 3:3–4: *"For what if some did not believe? Will their unbelief make the faithfulness of God without effect? Certainly not! Indeed, let God be true but every man a liar. As it is written: 'That You may be justified in Your words, And may overcome when You are judged.'"* (NKJV)

During His ministry, the Lord reproached the teachers of the law, the very same thing these apocrypha accomplish today in the lives of believers, in Luke 11:52. *"Woe to you lawyers! For you have taken away the key of knowledge. You did not enter yourselves, and you hindered those who were entering."* (ESV)

What these three stories have done so far is to cast doubt on the authenticity of the Bible and corroborate the rumor of its legendary origin. As sunlight that is hidden by a cloud cannot make plants sprout, so the glory of the Lord is obscured by this fog created by the enemies of our souls. They lead people to believe that the world is only material and not spiritual, to accept to be mistreated by pointing to bad luck, fate or coincidences to justify these misdeeds. And this is exactly what the "legends faction" wants, to act with impunity against victims, who accept their misfortune without even trying to fight back. Their major advantage is that more and more people are certain that the Bible and God, if they were authentic, could not help them, for the more lucid. For the rest, they're just legends. It's the same as giving up the ideal weapon that would change the balance of power in our favor. The myriad religions and currents of thought invented by the devil, have no other purpose than to guide those who follow them into a dead-end labyrinth, that offers nothing but the death of the soul.

Since the end of life on earth is certain, and words, thoughts and dreams prove the spiritual aspect of this life, to ignore this fact is to refuse to take one's existence into one's own hands, and give meaning to that which enables us to discover the real purpose of our journey on earth, as well as that long-sought freedom. In view of the countless truths and facts, not to mention the prophecies that bear witness to this day, it would be wise, however, for the sake of prudence, to pay attention to this persistent warning, before it turns into an unfortunate fact that could have been avoided: the test of everyone's faith is a certainty under the sun, and no one will escape it. By observing life around us, we can quickly realize that this reality is as certain as the limit of our existence here on earth. We need to educate ourselves while we're still breathing, because afterwards it won't be necessary. Then we'll be faced with the truth, and previous choices will have determined our eternity in bliss or torments. The time for choice and action is on earth, and that time is now. And if this is the time to put into practice what our life will be like in eternity, after our temporal existence, is there anything more important than this learning? That's why the Lord asks the question in Mark 8:36. *"For what does it profit a man to gain the whole world and forfeit his soul?"* (ESV) and Psalms 49:17 confirming *"For when he dies he shall carry nothing away; His glory shall not descend after him."* (ESV)

This physical life is a faculty that teaches us the right mindset to adopt before the Lord while serving Him. Ministry is the internship that allows us to practice the developed abilities. To be successful, we should listen to wisdom and learn from every interaction. For all is meant for a purpose, which is our life in eternal bliss.

The Bible, apart from these apocryphal books, remains God's Holy Word, Sovereign and capable of saving souls, just as God is in control of everything that's happening. When skipping these untrue accounts, the scriptures suddenly become a breeze, and everything just makes sense because coherence and consistency have been restored. The Bible is plain and simple enough to allow anyone to learn per their ability, then grow as they study and become erudite. As it enlightens the heart, the mind is changed to bring a new perspective of life. Just like the sun manifests life with the spring season, so much is the understanding of God's Word improving one's reasoning and changing one's habits to adopt those of the Lord Jesus Christ. Walking in love has everything to do with thinking just as the Lord does and putting it into practice day after day. There will be diverse kinds of adversities attempting to change our conduct, just like these false accounts and the corruption of the Church's leadership display. That will in no case change our determination as Christians to manifest God's Glory in this world according to His desire. The devil and his followers will launch manifold stratagems in an attempt to overthrow our faith in the Lord in quest of the perdition of our souls, but as the Lord said clearly in John 16:33, "*I have said these things to you, that in me you may have peace. In the world you will have tribulation. But take heart; I have overcome the world.*" (ESV)

Surely, many tricks will be used to convince one that the Bible isn't reliable and its insight useless. That just defends the apostle's prophecy in 2 Peter 3:3. "*. . . scoffers will come in the last* *days, walking according to their own lusts,"* (ESV)

God is of Peace and wants to save souls from damnation of eternal death, meaning He works at strengthening those who want to walk per His commandments. Anyone seeking the truth will bypass the various snares the devil's children keep bringing on our route. A study of the Scriptures allows one to discern, through the help of the Holy Spirit, what the intent of the writing is to bring it into its context to enlighten the reader's heart. The Lord said in John 17:25–26, *"O righteous Father, even though the world does not know you, I know you, and these know that you have sent me. I made known to them your name, and I will continue to make it known, that the love with which you have loved me may be in them, and I in them."* (ESV)

Through the Holy Spirit, the reader is ushered in all the truth of the Almighty God and discovers the numerous treasures of wisdom and knowledge hidden in Christ Jesus. Note that the Holy Spirit is not a voice that we hear and that dictates our conduct. This is a maneuver of the enemy to lead God's children astray. We walk by faith, that is, we apply what is written in the Bible. God gives us wisdom through His Holy Spirit, so that we understand His Word perfectly. So, it's an enhanced perception that we develop, as we explore the Holy Scriptures. Just like nobody can learn the various deceits used with counterfeit money, studying the original in all its smaller details allows one to spot the counterfeited currency by seeing its defects. Likewise, knowing God's Word allows one to debunk false teachings, including the doctrine of demons and the various machinations of the "legends faction" launched to discredit the Holy Word of the Almighty God. Simply because one who is acquainted with the truth has adopted the Lord's mind, they will become uncomfortable when faced with mischiefs, and on top of that, their reasoning will expose all hidden, diverse lies' perversions. The more our faith grows, the more its expansion reveals the hidden workings of the enemies of our souls, in our daily lives and through our trials.

The more it increases, the more blatant the attacks become, as the enemy has fewer and fewer resources with which to hide his misdeeds; growth in the knowledge of the truth pushes him back into his last ramparts. Perseverance in learning the truth is therefore the key to salvation.

Knowing the truth grants assurance, and stirs the confidence to grow even more in a knowledge that's infinite. If the Lord said to be courageous, it's because everything will be done to derail our faith. However, we can see in Revelation 2 and 3, even in churches that have bad conduct, are faithful believers that will walk with the Lord, as reads Revelation 3:1: "*And to the angel of the church in Sardis write: The words of him who has the seven spirits of God and the seven stars. I know your works. You have the reputation of being alive, but you are dead.*" (ESV)

Though this church is rebuked by the Lord, verses 3:4–5 however, reveal the following: "*Yet you have still a few names in Sardis, people who have not soiled their garments, and they will walk with me in white, for they are worthy. The one who conquers will be clothed thus in white garments, and I will never blot his name out of the book of life. I will confess his name before my Father and before his angels.*" (ESV)

This is not an invite to abide in a dead church; it proves, however, that God is in control and sees each one's deeds, which will be retributed accordingly before the Throne of Grace. The aim pursued on earth will be recompensed.

Like a building raised on a good or bad foundation will stand or fall, so is human existence nourished with truth or lies, even the soul of man. And just as the detective's skill and the lawyer's acumen strengthen any case in court, so is Bible study for faith, before trials arise and test one's knowledge of the truth. Nothing is done in vain, as God searches the hearts of all. The appraisal we'll receive will accurately represent a work expressing the true and intrinsic nature of each one of us. There won't be partiality which means no favoritism.

Therefore, in conclusion: Consider reading the Bible

without these three books for a while. Then go back and read them again, and experience the discomfort that such confusion causes. Once you are convinced, stay away from these scriptures forever, and you will grow considerably in the knowledge of the truth. Don't take my word for it, but experience it for yourself and be convinced that our battle is truly against evil forces in the heavenly realms; the truth is unique and unchangeable, as the Lord clearly said in Luke 21:33. *"Heaven and earth shall pass away, but my words shall not pass away."* (ESV)

The Holy Word of God remains the truth, and its power is still the same, just as it was in apostolic times, and even from eternity. God doesn't change. It will be revealed to those who worship in Spirit and in truth, which implies an absence of paganism found in just about every denomination today. God doesn't need all the bells and whistles this world has to offer, but only our hearts that are sincere and fully dedicated to following His Word: Since understanding is to turn away from the evil of this world, we must demonstrate wisdom by fearing the Lord.

Let us then worship according to the truth through the Spirit of Jesus Christ, and reap the many blessings God has prepared for His people.

ABOUT THE AUTHOR

Regis Eitel N. is a living proof of the Bible's authenticity. Just as it is written that disciples will be persecuted for the Name of the Lord, so his life has been. From his early childhood until today, he's faced numerous challenges that prove the importance of his faith in Jesus Christ.

Recently, he became the survivor of a devastating storm that destroyed all aspects of his life. Instead of being crushed and in total despair despite losing family, friends, job, and even his health, he has mutated into a prolific writer whose honesty continues to challenge the status quo.

Although "Holdup On Holiness" is the first book to be self-published through his company, Eitel Media Inc., it is actually the third of four manuscripts he has completed.

With a long background in business relations, he founded Eitel Media Inc. to self-publish and promote his work. His natural creativity allows him to play various instruments and sing for the Lord, which is one of the many upcoming projects the company will be undertaking. Stay tuned!

To follow his work:

www.eitelmedia.com

AFTERWORD

At the time this manuscript was about to be published, I was involved in a bicycle accident and broke my right collarbone. This incident is only one of a long list of events that have prevented me from publishing my books, as well as from producing the songs that I have already written and for some of which I have even recorded a demo version. It's been ten years of postponement for various reasons, all having in common the delay of my testimony of God's love and Faithfulness. Is all this pure coincidence that has created the life of chaos that I've been a victim of?

I went to see a doctor who told me how many of his patients tell him they're no longer depressed; are we experiencing a pandemic of this disease, or is this an ignored sign of the tribulation that is hitting upright ones? Considering the novel coronavirus known as Covid-19, which has affected nations around the world, and threw many companies out of business while others have thrived and never been more successful. Coincidence?

Without diving in conspiracy theories, it's however obvious that a worldwide purge is taking place, and many who don't abide by this world's culture are making the most of these casualties observed in this tumultuous economic season. If Russia's war in Eastern Europe against Ukraine has set off a chain reaction whose secondary effects continue to shatter the livelihoods of many communities around the world, other social inequalities complete the work of eliminating the most vulnerable, even those whose views differ from those of this world. Silently and with no apparent purpose or causality, people from different backgrounds are thrown to the margins of society, with the only option for restoration being the surrender of their integrity.

Nevertheless, I continue to follow the Lord's path - even as I type these words with my left hand, despite being right-handed and working slowly - because the way of love is much more rewarding than any other alternative.

Existence could be thought of as a timetable with distinct slots for different activities. If indeed our sufferings are to last our lifetime on earth, our reward in heaven with the Lord will last longer, even as much as time can no longer be counted. A wise man described earthly activities in these simple words:

"For everything there is a season, and a time for every matter under heaven." (ESV) (Ecclesiastes 3:1)

ACKNOWLEDGEMENTS

First and foremost, I would like to thank the Almighty God, Father of the Lord Jesus Christ, for giving me the wisdom and inspiration to write this book. Many times, I have written things that were beyond my knowledge and understanding, only to realize afterwards the depth and genuineness of the explanation. Therefore, in all humility, I must admit that what has been produced, if done through me, is not my wisdom. I may not have delivered the exactness of the message, but I certainly brought the essence and did my best to deliver what was given to me.

It is obvious that some circumstances are special and not appropriate for a project of this magnitude, but are there really some that are appropriate? We are living in strange times, a period of transition marked by upheavals that impose the need to adapt quickly and provide others with the useful information that an original setup implies. Romans 12:6-13 sums up my logic. *"Having gifts that differ according to the grace given to us, let us use them: (…) Contribute to the needs of the saints …"* (ESV)

I would also like to thank all those who have crossed my path and whose influence, good or bad, in my life has contributed to the production of this book. Although most people were hostile in many ways, I was still able to learn from these interactions and God gave me the knowledge and wisdom that culminated in this book. Romans 8:28 says, *"… all things work together for good to those who love God, to those who are called according to His purpose."* (ESV)

O Heavenly Father, I thank You Lord my God, for Your Grace and Mercy. If words are too weak to express my gratitude for the countless blessings that have marked my life since my earliest childhood, the joy of growing a little more in the knowledge of my Savior each time is simply indescribable. In truth, Your love is really boundless and unconditional. In fact, the whole world can turn against me, as I have experienced for well over ten years now, I remain calm because the One who is in my heart is stronger than all. I thank You for the privilege You have given me to rise up and make truth triumph. I entrust this venture into Your Hands that only Your Will be done and that all glory be given to You. I pray in the Holy, Glorious, Powerful and Everlasting Name of Jesus Christ, my Lord and Savior. Amen!

To the reader, a heartfelt thank you for taking the time to read this book. I hope it brings you the enlightenment you are seeking with the abundance of blessings promised by Almighty God.

If you enjoyed its content, would you please consider leaving an honest review on the platform where you purchased this book? This will help spread the word by making it more visible and accessible to others. Thanks in advance!

ASSISTANCE

Thank you again for taking the time to discover this book. I really hope you found it interesting and perhaps an eye opener? Would you be kind enough to write an honest review on the platform where you purchased it? It makes a huge difference in spreading the word by making the book more discoverable. It would be greatly appreciated if you could take the time to do this.

Have you enjoyed the book and would you like to help?

Would you please take the time to pray for me, and ask the Lord Jesus Christ to strengthen His servant, by giving him such determination that he can continue to endure the various tribulations, and do all that He wants him to do for the glory of His Holy Name. More than anything else, prayers are what I really need at this time.

Perhaps you would like to help in another way?

Your support and words of encouragement when sharing your opinion of the book on social media, or when writing a review are really helpful and make a huge difference.

You've been convinced by the various pieces of evidence and would like to help?

Please don't hesitate to share your copy of the book or simply recommend it to someone else. Making people aware of the deception that these three books inserted into the Bible represent will definitely save many souls by allowing people to understand God's Word without the confusion that these Apocrypha bring.

Any way possible to help spread the word and raise awareness of this forgery would certainly help and the Faithful Witness in Heaven, our Lord and Saviour Jesus Christ, will certainly reward those who stand up for His Holy Name, no matter how small the action.

Warmest regards,
Regis Eitel N.

COPYRIGHTS

The following versions of the Holy Bible were quoted in this book, according to their respective copyright rules:

English Standard Version (ESV)

Revised Version (RV) or English Revised Version (ERV)

International Standard Version (ISV)

King James Version (KJV)

Public Domain

Literal Standard Version (LSV)

New American Standard Bible / Version (NASB)

New King James Version (NKJV)

BIBLIOGRAPHY

The following books are available for free consultation on the Archive.org and some of them can be found on Wikipedia.org

1.   **Contra Celsum**
The Writings of Origen - Origen, Against Celsus,
(AD 185 to 253)

O light and truth! He distinctly declares, with his own voice, as ye yourselves have recorded, that there will come to you even others, employing miracles of a similar kind, who are wicked men, and sorcerers; and Satan. So that Jesus himself does not deny that these works at least are not at all divine, but are the acts of wicked men; and being compelled by the force of truth, he at the same time not only laid open the doings of others, but convicted himself of the same acts. Is it not, then, a miserable inference, to conclude from the same works that the one is God and the other sorcerers? Why ought the others, because of these acts, to be accounted wicked rather than this man, seeing they have him as their witness against himself? For he has himself acknowledged that these are not the works of a divine nature, but the inventions of certain deceivers, and of thoroughly wicked men.

2.   **Antiquities of the Jews**
The Writings of Flavius Josephus (born Yosef ben Matityahu),
(AD 37 to about 100)

There was about this time Jesus, a wise man, if it be lawful to call him a man, for he was a doer of wonderful works—a teacher of such men as receive the truth with pleasure. He drew over to him both many of the Jews, and many of the Gentiles. He was Christ; and when Pilate, at the suggestion of the principal men amongst us, had condemned him to the cross, those that loved him at the first did not forsake him, for he appeared to them alive again the third day, as the divine prophets had foretold these and ten thousand other wonderful things concerning him; and the tribe of Christians, so named from him, are not extinct at this day (Antiquities 18:3:3).

Festus was now dead, and Albinus was but upon the road; so he [Ananus] assembled the Sanhedrin of judges, and brought before them the brother of Jesus, who was called Christ, whose name was James, and some others; and when he had formed an accusation against them as breakers of the law, he delivered them to be stoned (Antiquities 20:9:1).

3.   Annals
The Writings of Tacitus, (AD 56 to 120)

Consequently, to get rid of the report, Nero fastened the guilt and inflicted the most exquisite tortures on a class hated for their abominations, called Christians by the populace. Christus, from whom the name had its origin, suffered the extreme penalty during the reign of Tiberius at the hands of one of our procurators, Pontius Pilatus, and a most mischievous superstition, thus checked for the moment, again broke out not only in Judæa, the first source of the evil, but even in Rome, where all things hideous and shameful from every part of the world find their centre and become popular. Accordingly, an arrest was first made of all who pleaded guilty; then, upon their information, an immense multitude was convicted, not so much of the crime of firing the city, as of hatred against mankind.

4.   Epistles 10.96
The Writings of Pliny the Younger, (AD 62 to 113)

They (Christians) were in the habit of meeting on a certain fixed day before it was light, when they sang in alternate verses a hymn to Christ, as to a god, and bound themselves by a solemn oath, not to any wicked deeds, but never to commit any fraud, theft or adultery, never to falsify their word, nor deny a trust when they should be called upon to deliver it up; after which it was their custom to separate, and then reassemble to partake of food, but of an ordinary and innocent kind (Epistles 10.96).

5.   The Passing of Peregrinus
The Writings of Lucian of Samosata, (AD 125 to 180)

The Christians, you know, worship a man to this day—the distinguished personage who introduced their novel rites, and was crucified on that account. … You see, these misguided creatures start with the general conviction that they are immortal for all time, which explains their contempt of death and voluntary self-devotion which are so common among them; and then it was impressed on them by their original lawgiver that they are all brothers, from the moment that they are converted, and deny the gods of Greece, and worship the crucified sage, and live after his laws. All this they take quite on faith, with the result that they despise all worldly goods alike, regarding them merely as common property. (Lucian, The Passing of Peregrinus)

6.   **Ecclesiastical History**
The writings of Eusebius, Bishop of Caesarea,
(AD 260 to 340)
Eusebius provides accounts of various persecutions and the steadfastness of Christians in the face of death.

7.   **The Apostolic Fathers**
With Justin Martyr and Irenaeus, ed. Roberts, Donaldson, and Coxe, vol. 1

8.   **The Ante-Nicene Fathers**
Christian Literature Company, 1885, p. 155

9.   **Fat Chance**
By Robert H. Lustig
Lustig, a pediatric endocrinologist, explains how sugar affects our hormones and contributes to obesity and other health issues.

10.   **The Case Against Sugar**
By Gary Taubes
This book explores the history of sugar consumption and its impact on health, arguing that sugar is a major contributor to many chronic diseases.

The excerpts used in the bibliography of this book come from the sources below. Although included in the bibliography, the author does not endorse the ideology or beliefs of these groups.

Sources: 1 to 6 from aleteia.org; 7 to 8 from gotquestion.org